The Growing Difference

Natural Success Through Horticultural-Based Programming

By
Pam Catlin

Susan ~
Thank you for
the difference you
make! Pam

Cover and interior design by Genna Herron.

ACKNOWLEDGEMENTS

This manual went beyond the dream stage and into reality largely due to support from the late Susan J. Rheem. Susan, founder and executive director of Adult Care Services, Inc. (ACS), along with the team of staff and consultants, included the project in a grant proposal to the Emerald Foundation. The requested funding was awarded and the work began. Susan had been a proponent of horticultural therapy even before I met her in 1991, and she continued to promote the work up until her passing in 2011.

I have deep gratitude for the on-going encouragement from my husband, Tom, and many friends and colleagues, despite how long it took me to complete the project. Jentle Harts Consulting played an important role in obtaining the grant funding. They also provided guidance, person-centered care editing, and good fellowship. A special thank you to friend and past volunteer, Lucia Murphy who, a decade ago, thought it would be a great idea to put these activities into a book for others to use. Her initial vision was the first step toward creating *The Growing Difference*.

This book is a collection of ideas implemented during my years of working in the field of horticultural therapy. I would like to acknowledge the many registered horticultural therapists in the American Horticultural Therapy Association who have created successful interventions over the years. They have inspired and transformed numerous lives through this wonderful medium of plants. Even prior to my employment (1986-1991) with Chicago Botanic Garden (CBG), CBG's Horticultural Therapy Services made a difference in my career. The early manuals produced by CBG, were my "go-to" books for developing programs during my start-up years in the field, and the organization continues to be renowned for its work.

Thanks also to Susan Crutcher, Carol Hunter-Geboy and Peter Powers for their editing help, and Genna Herron for her graphics expertise, excellent photography and guidance through the publishing process.

CONTENTS

CHAPTER 1

AN INTRODUCTION TO HORTICULTURAL-BASED ACTIVITIES

Why Was This Book Written?

After 30-plus years of listening to volunteers and students saying, "You should put these ideas into a book," and receiving funding assistance through a grant from the Emerald Foundation, a dream of mine has finally come into being.

Throughout my years of working as a registered horticultural therapist, I have seen what I can only call "miracles" through the use of horticultural-based projects. The activities in this book have all been successfully used with a variety of populations. It is clear that people of all ages and abilities have an innate love of nature. It is my intention that this guide be useful in assisting others to take the first steps toward adding a horticultural/nature component to programs serving people with special needs, or to be used as an enrichment dimension in wellness programs.

From the beginning of my career, I have observed that engaging in structured, yet flexible, horticultural-based interventions resulted in relaxed and therapeutically productive sessions for participants. I have looked at this with great interest, amazement and satisfaction. The plant world is, without a doubt, a doorway to enrichment possibilities for any age, any gender, any ability.

To help create success through the nature connection this book provides:
- Structured horticultural activities to incorporate into an existing program or practice.
- The required time, materials and step-by-step directions for each activity.
- Potential outcomes/goals for use in care plans, individual program plans, or individual education plans.
- Adaptive and expansion suggestions for many of the activities.
- Resources for obtaining further support information.

What are Horticultural-Based Activities?

Horticultural-based activities are multi-sensory activities designed to help people of all ages develop their sensory, motor, cognitive, communication, and social skills. Emotional benefits and physical benefits may be derived from these activities, as well. Although well planned out, they are flexible, and provide opportunities for spontaneous, natural and meaningful interactions with the environment. The person and "their process" is the focal point during these sessions. The plants and projects simply serve as the tools used to help individuals and groups reach their goals and objectives.

What Are The Characteristics Of Horticultural-Based Activities?

Horticultural-based activities are distinctive for a variety of reasons. Because they are directly related to nature, they are engaging, easily adaptable, safe, present a high likelihood for success, and still develop functional skills, which can be generalized into daily activities. The following expands on these characteristics:

- **Engaging:** Individuals enjoy participating in activities which assist them in interacting with nature and their environment and also encourage creativity.
- **Easily Adaptable:** All activities are designed for flexibility; therefore, they may be adapted to meet the needs of the multiple-ability levels of the participants.
- **High Rate of Success:** Active learners who are provided with interesting and functionally appropriate projects are led to success.
- **Functional Skill/Generalizing:** All domains are interrelated. Development in one area directly affects the development in other domains. Research indicates skills can be developed more effectively in our natural environment, and these skills tend to generalize across different settings (Warren & Kaiser, 1986).
- **Safe:** Safety is always a primary concern when working with individuals and groups in every setting. No toxic or harmful plants or substances are to be used. If an individual or group cannot safely use scissors or knives, that portion of the activity should be adapted. Information on non-poisonous and poisonous plants can be found in Appendix I, page 160.

What Are Some Advantages of a Horticultural-Based Activity?

There are many advantages to utilizing a horticultural-based activity:
- It can be used in a group setting, yet individual goals and objectives can be easily addressed.
- It can be effective for home-based, community-based or individual intervention.
- It provides a safe means for individuals to interact with their environment.
- It is compatible with the multi-disciplinary approach used by many professionals.

CHAPTER 2

ACTIVITIES FOR USE THROUGHOUT THE YEAR

How To Use This Manual

This manual is written based on the understanding that a person's process is the main product versus the material item that is made and taken away. The activities in this book are created with a number of individual and/or group goals in mind. Most of the projects are written to cover general goals held by a variety of populations. Objectives can be developed from the directed tasks to meet more specific needs.

The following is an example of developing an objective based on the goals and directions listed: One of the goals in the activity *Transplanting Time* is to maintain/improve fine motor skills. In the directions, there are at least four steps that require participants to use fine motor skills.

An objective then might be: *Participant will use their fine motor skills in a supervised planting process for at least ten minutes.* This is a measurable objective that also specifies how the participant will incorporate their motor skills. More information on goals and objectives can be found in Appendix F, page 156.

In addition to client/resident goals, there are program goals. One such goal would be *To develop a congruent program that incorporates horticultural resources in a meaningful way* (Haller, Kramer, 2006). This refers to creating a program that builds upon itself. If specific plants or plant materials are needed for one activity, an earlier activity will produce those items. For more specific help, go to the Index of Activity Plans, page 4.

For ease of use, most of the plant names used in the session plans are common names. For plants whose common names are less familiar than the botanic name, the latter is used. Both common and botanic names are listed in Appendix N, Plant Names As Used In Manual, page 170.

Each activity in the manual provides the following information:
- Time needed for the activity
- Goal areas addressed
- Materials required
- Planning notes & precautions
- Step-by-step instruction
- Helpful hints to enhance the presentation of the activity and provide for optimal success, such as:
    Vocabulary
    Concepts
    Points of interest
    Adaptations
    Pages for notes

INDEX OF ACTIVITY PLANS

NATURE ART

Notes

Sand Art Decorations

⏲ Time Allowed: 60 minutes

Materials:
- Sample of project
- One clear plastic drink cup per person
- One stir stick per person
- Three colors of bagged decorator sand
- Small paper cups or plastic scoops (four per person)
- Selection of dried flowers
- School glue diluted with water and placed in cups or scoops for pouring
- Water-proof markers

Precautions:
✓ Monitor participants with cognitive impairments closely to avoid any chance of ingesting the materials.
  Do not use this project with those who have high levels of confusion.

Planning Notes:
✓ Purchase colored sand or, if making your own, purchase salt and colored chalk (follow directions on Helpful Hints page).
✓ Prepare cups of sand prior to start of session.
  Use scoops instead of cups for groups with cognitive impairment.
✓ Either raise your own straw flowers and statice or purchase at craft store.
✓ Prepare thinned glue in advance.

Sand Art Decoration

Step-by-Step Directions

1. Show a finished project and initiate discussion about the art of sand painting and the various cultures that work with it (see Helpful Hints on next page).
2. Pass around the selection of dried flowers/plants for all to feel and, if they were grown on site, reminisce about how and where they were grown.
3. Hand out clear cups and a waterproof marker and have each person write his/her name on the bottom of the cup.
4. Distribute the small containers of sand to each person.
5. Pour cup/scoop of one color of sand into a clear plastic cup.
6. Repeat with second color of sand.
7. Place stir stick against inside of the cup and push straight down, creating a design in the sand.
   * Repeat Step 7 until the desired design has been created.
8. Pour in third color of sand.
9. Repeat Step 7.
10. Continue filling the clear cup with sand until about ¼-inch from the top of the cup.
11. Distribute dried flowers.
12. Create a dried flower arrangement by pushing the stems of the selected dried materials into the sand, one at a time.
13. Pour thinned glue over sand until all of the sand surface is covered.
    * *The glue will dry to a hard surface in approximately one day.*

Sand Art Decoration

Helpful Hints

Concepts:

• Sand painting.

Points of Interest:

• Many cultures utilize the art of sand painting.
• A variety of colors make up the desert landscape.

Adaptations:

✓ A small succulent can be planted in a cup that is then placed into the center of the clear cup prior to adding any sand. Secure the planter cup to the clear cup with a softened ball of floral clay to ensure it will stay in position.

✓ Instead of colored sand, salt can be colored and used. Rub colored chalk over course sand paper and collect the powdered color. Stir the powdered chalk into a container of salt. Repeat with clean salt for as many colors as you desire. This could be turned into an extra facet of the project that would utilize upper gross and fine motor skills and tactile sensation.

Cedar Sachets

⏱ **Time Allowed:** 45 minutes

Goal Areas:
Sensory
Fine Motor
Cognitive
Social/Emotional

Planning Notes:
- ✓ Create a sample prior to session.
- ✓ Purchase cedar shavings at a pet supply store.
- ✓ Either purchase muslin bags or make them in a previous session.

Materials:
- Sample of project
- Fresh cedar greenery and seed pods
- Cotton muslin or burlap sachet bags
- Ink pads and stamps (optional)
- Plastic spoons
- Bowls
- Sprigs of fresh cedar (optional)
- Cedar shavings
- Variety of colored ribbons
- Craft glue, glue plates and spreading sticks
- Variety of silk and/or strawflowers
- Tape and markers
- Scissors

Precautions:
- ✓ Count scissors before, during and after session.

Cedar Sachets

Step-by-Step Directions

1. Open with discussion of the cedar tree and show samples of the greenery and the seeds. You may want to include discussion suggestions (see Helpful Hints on next page).

2. Show sample of the project.

3. Give each person a sachet bag. The bag can be made of either muslin or burlap. Or, (an option that provides more steps) give each person a muslin sachet bag and a selection of stamps and ink pads.

   a. Demonstrate how to make a design on the bag by pressing the stamp on the ink pad and then stamping the bag.

   b. Have each person decorate their bags using the stamps and ink.

4. Provide each person with a container of cedar shavings and a spoon, and guide them through the following steps.

   a. Using the spoon, fill the bag with the shavings.

   b. When the bag is full, tie the bag closed with ribbon, inserting a sprig of cedar while tying (see picture on previous page).

5. Place a generous spot of glue on the knot of the ribbon bow or elsewhere on the bag where a flower is desired.

   * Place strawflower or artificial flower on the glue.

6. Label with names written on a piece of tape.

7. Discuss what to do with completed sachets.

Cedar Sachets

Helpful Hints

Concepts:
- Natural control of moths.
- Cedar wood has natural preservatives.
- Common uses of cedar:
  * Cedar closets
  * Cedar chests
  * Cedar sachets
  * Pet beds
  * Cedar siding
  * Jewelry (seeds)
  * Crafts (seed pods)
  * Raised bed planters

Points of Interest:
- Cedar shavings can be purchased in pet stores.
- Cedar trees are common in the forests of Western Washington and Oregon.
- The Jewish holiday, *Tu Bishvat*, utilizes cedar and cypress.

Adaptations:
- ✓ For groups with good fine motor dexterity, sewing the bags could be part of the project.
- ✓ For groups who have compromised fine motor skills, adaptations could be made, such as using a small cup to scoop instead of the spoon and providing assistance with the ribbon tying.
- ✓ For those with the use of only one hand or challenges with fine motor skills, place the open bag in a cup to hold it upright and tape the cup to the table to prevent it from tipping over.

Notes

Valentine Pomanders

⏰ Time Allowed: 60 minutes

Goal Areas:
Sensory
Fine Motor
Cognitive
Social/Emotional

Materials:
- Sample of project
- One small papier-mâché heart per person
- Paint brush for each person
- Small bowls
- Water
- Wet rags or hand wipes
- Finely pulverized potpourri or herbs such as lavender
- Waxed paper
- Thin non-latex gloves
- Aprons
- Thin white glue
- Water-proof markers

Precautions:
✓ Do not do this project with those who have compromised breathing.
✓ Some potpourris can cause skin reactions. Always wear gloves when handling.

Planning Notes:
✓ Make sample in advance.
✓ Purchase potpourri if not made in an earlier session.
✓ Pulverize potpourri in blender.
✓ Thin glue with water in advance.

Valentine Pomanders

Step-by-Step Directions

1. Prior to handing out materials, have discussion about Valentine's Day and encourage participants to share memories regarding the holiday. Following discussion, show a sample of the finished project and also talk about potpourri (see Helpful Hints on next page for Points of Interest).
2. Provide each participant with a sheet of waxed paper, gloves, bowl of glue, brush, wet towel, and heart.
3. Have participants:
    a. Put on gloves.
    b. Brush glue over the heart covering completely (see Helpful Hints on next page for Adaptations).
    c. When the heart is covered with glue, gently roll it in potpourri.
    d. When the heart is completely covered with potpourri, lay it on a clean sheet of waxed paper to dry.
    e. Write name on waxed paper with marker for later identification.

Helpful Hints

Concepts:

- What is potpourri?

Points of Interest:

- The word potpourri means "rotten pot" in French.
- Potpourri jars -- opaque, with a solid cover to keep scent in and a pierced cover to let it out – may date back a few hundred years.
- "Strewing herbs" were used in the middle ages to sweeten the air.
- Dry potpourri is usually fortified with essential oils, and essential oils go back at least to the late middle ages.
- It has been reported that jars of rose petals have been excavated from ancient sites in Egypt.

Adaptations:

- ✓ For those challenged in using a brush, glue could be poured into a deeper bowl and the heart could be dipped to cover it with glue.
- ✓ This project could be done with shapes other than hearts if not wanting a Valentine's theme.
- ✓ Expand this to two sessions by creating an activity plan to make the potpourri. There are many recipes available online and in herb books.

Notes

Picture Perfect Pots

⏱ Time Allowed: 45 minutes

Goal Areas:
Sensory
Fine Motor
Upper Gross Motor
Cognitive
Social/Emotional

Materials:
- Sample of project
- Two 16-oz. plastic cups per person
- Paint brushes
- Small containers for decoupage
- Non-toxic decoupage
- Collection of flower/nature pictures cut to 1- to 2-inch size
- Water-proof markers
- Masking tape
- Cup of warm, soapy water
- Aprons
- Hand wipes or disposable non-latex gloves
- Plastic table coverings or waxed paper

Precautions:
✓ The decoupage does not easily wash out of clothing once dried Wipe off any spills immediately.
✓ Only use decoupage that is labeled "non-toxic."
✓ If working with individuals with severe cognitive impairment, avoid using drinking cups to hold the decoupage.

Planning Notes:
✓ Create the sample a day or more in advance.
✓ Prepare pictures in advance, possibly in an earlier session.

Picture Perfect Pots

Step-by-Step Directions

1. Either cover tables with plastic or lay down a placemat-sized sheet of waxed paper for each person.
2. Show a sample of the project explaining how each person is going to decorate a cup that will serve as a pot for a plant in a later session.
3. Provide each person with a cup.
4. Have those that are able, write names on the cup bottom (see Helpful Hints on next page for adaptation).
5. Hand out a container of decoupage and a brush to each person and give the following instructions:
   a. Place non-dominant hand inside the cup (see Helpful Hints on next page for adaptation).
   b. Holding a paint brush in dominant hand, paint on a coat of decoupage until the cup is white.
   c. Place pictures onto sticky surface of cup.
   d. Encourage group to identify pictures.
   e. Paint another coat of decoupage over the pictures.
7. Place used brushes in a cup of soapy water.
8. Set the cups in a safe place to dry for at least 24 hours before using.

Helpful Hints

Concepts:

- Decoupage dries clear and serves as a protective coat. The more that is applied, the shinier it is.

Points of Interest:

- Decoupage is used in many craft projects as a means of adding "shine," as well as protecting the pictures underneath.
- The "Mod Podge" brand of decoupage is non-toxic.

Adaptations:

✓ For those with the use of only one hand:
  a. Tape the cup to a flat piece of cardboard the size of a placemat so it will not move.
  b. Have the participant paint half of the cup, put on the pictures and cover with a coat of decoupage.
  c. When complete with one side, turn the cardboard mat to do the opposite side.

✓ For anyone unable to write, pre-print names on masking tape and have the individuals stick the tape to the cup bottom.

✓ For those with minimal fine motor skills, a "universal cuff" might be used to hold the paint brush. This requires only upper gross motor movement which can be more easily assisted by the facilitator or volunteer.

Notes

Sun Pictures

⏲ **Time Allowed:** 60 minutes

Goal Areas:
Sensory
Fine Motor
Cognitive
Language
Social/Emotional

Materials:
- Sample of project
- Solar paper (available at specialty education supply stores and S&S catalogue)
- Pencils
- Collection of appropriate plant materials
- Cookie trays
- Sheets of clear plexi-glass no bigger than cookie trays
- Large bowls or trays of water
- Paper towels
- Iron
- Glue sticks
- Card stock or construction paper
- Envelopes
- Aprons (optional)

Precautions:
✓ Closely monitor any participant-use of the hot iron.
✓ The water used for developing the picture can stain clothing. Avoid splashing or dripping.

Planning Notes:
✓ Set up for session indoors or in a well shaded location.
✓ Have leaves, flowers, etc., picked prior to start of session.
✓ The sun takes a picture of the shape presented. If plant materials are placed on top of each other, the picture will just show up as a blob.

Sun Pictures

Step-by-Step Directions

1. This project requires full sun for one step, yet most of the steps must be done indoors or in full shade. Show completed project to the group and discuss the process.
2. Distribute one piece of solar paper to each person, blue side down.
3. Have each participant write his/her name on the white side of the paper.
4. Provide each person with a collection of suitable flowers/foliage (see Helpful Hints on next page for suggestions).
5. Encourage each person to create a design by placing flowers/foliage face down on the blue side of the paper. Point out that the design is for shape only, not color.
6. When designs are complete, move papers to a cookie tray and cover with clear plexi-glass. Place covered trays outdoors in the sun until the paper turns white (1 to 2 minutes).
7. Bring the tray of papers back inside.
8. Re-distribute to each person with instructions to remove the plant material from page.
9. Place papers upside down in water for 1 minute.
10. Remove papers from water and place between paper towels to blot.
11. Finish drying by ironing paper with a dry iron.
12. Glue the dried, flattened picture on to folded cardstock or construction paper.

Sun Pictures

Helpful Hints

Concepts:
- How blueprint paper works.
- How does sunlight go through some colors such as yellow and white?

Points of Interest:
- The best flowers and foliage are those whose petals and leaves have low-moisture content. When using composite flowers (have a thick center) individual petals need to be used. Do not use white flowers as they do not block the sun. Suggested flowers are:
  * Marigolds – petals and foliage
  * Nierembergia – flowers and foliage
  * Geraniums – flowers
  * Verbena – individual flowers
  * Dusty miller – foliage
  * Scented geranium foliage with interesting margins
  * Locust – foliage
  * Ferns
- The pictures will darken as they dry.
- The sun paper is similar to what architects use for blueprint paper.
- If you try to do these outdoors and do not have full shade, the paper will develop while being worked on and the picture will not be clear.

Adaptations
- ✓ People with minimal vision can be encouraged to use their tactile senses to note where the plant materials are placed.
- ✓ For individuals with progressed forms of memory loss, offer a smaller selection of plant items to help reduce confusion with the process.

Notes

Pounded Petals Picture

⏱ Time Allowed: 45 minutes

Goal Areas:
Sensory
Fine Motor
Gross Motor
Social/Emotional

Materials:
- Sample of project
- Cross-stitch cloth or muslin
- Hammers and/or rounded stones
- Hard surfaces to pound on: table, cutting boards
- Selection of garden flowers/ foliage
- Embroidery hoops
- Sharp scissors
- Paper towels

Precautions:
- ✓ This creates too much stimulation for those with advanced memory loss or those with sensory issues.
- ✓ Always have direct supervision when using the hammers.
- ✓ Count scissors before, during and after session.

Planning Notes:
- ✓ Experiment ahead of time to select the best flowers and foliage to use and to make sample.
- ✓ Due to the noise level, this is an outdoor project only.

Pounded Petals Picture

Step-by-Step Directions

This is a project for outdoors due to the high noise level.

1. Show a sample of the project and demonstrate to the group each step.
2. When completed, identify the flowers and foliage used.
3. Distribute a fabric piece and a collection of suitable flowers/foliage (see Helpful Hints on next page for suggestions) to each person.
4. Place an embroidery hoop on top of fabric.
5. Create a design by placing flowers/foliage face down on the fabric within the hoop.
6. When satisfied with the design, remove the hoop and cover flowers with a paper towel.
7. At a table just for the step of pounding, place the fabric with the covered flowers on a cutting board or other hard surface.
8. Using a hammer or rounded stone, pound firmly over covered plants, being sure that each plant part gets pounded.
9. When the entire design is showing on the paper towel, stop pounding.
10. Remove paper towel and gently scrape plant material off of the cloth.
11. Place the fabric with the design back in the embroidery hoop. Center the picture and tighten the hoop.
12. Trim edges.

Pounded Petals Picture

Helpful Hints

Concepts:
- Plant dyes.

Points of Interest:
- Aida cloth (used for counted cross stitch) provides a "crisper" picture than muslin. Muslin provides more of a water color effect.
- The best flowers and foliage are those that do not have too much moisture in them. When using composite flowers (have a thick center) individual petals need to be used. Suggested flowers are:
  * Marigolds
  * Nierembergia
  * Geraniums, especially in shades of pink
  * Verbena
- If kept out of direct sun, these pictures will last many years.
- Years ago, prior to chemical dyes, fabric was often colored using natural materials.

Adaptations:
✓ If your budget does not allow for embroidery hoops, you can make cards, bookmarks or pictures by cutting material to the desired size and gluing the completed piece to construction paper (see picture on page 27).
✓ T-shirts and cloth bags can be printed on and then sprayed with a fixative that will allow the items to be washed without losing the decoration.

Preserving Flowers & Leaves

🕐 **Time Allowed:** 45 minutes

Goal Areas:
Sensory
Fine Motor
Cognitive
Language
Social/Emotional

Materials:
- Actual or pictures of pressed flower art
- Selection of freshly cut flowers and leaves (see Helpful Hints on page 33)
- Phone books
- Scrap paper
- Pens
- Heavy bricks or books
- Scissors
- Silica sand
- Aluminum or plastic containers with lids

Precautions:
✓ Skip the silica drying with any population that might ingest materials.
✓ Always count scissors before, during and after session.

Planning Notes:
✓ Prior to session either create or find pictures of pressed flower art.
✓ Pick fresh flowers immediately before using and place in plastic bag or container. These can be kept in a refrigerator for one day, if necessary.

Preserving Flowers & Leaves

Step-by-Step Directions

1.   Start the session by showing examples of pressed flower art and preserved floral decorations.

2.   Introduce the two methods used to preserve flowers/leaves for these types of projects.

3.   Explain that two teams will be formed to actually carry out these two processes. The preserved flowers/leaves will be used for projects in the future.

* **Group A: Pressing**
    a.   Provide each person with a page from a phone book and freshly cut flowers and/or leaves.
    b.   Ask each person to place the flowers or leaves, colorful side down, and in rows on the paper with space between each flower or leaf.
    c.   When the page is full, mark with a piece of paper that specifies what is on the page, and the date.
    d.   Place completed pages in phone book and cover with a heavy weight, such as bricks or books. Store in a dry place.
    e.   Flowers will be ready for use in two to three weeks.

* **Group B: Drying** (not for those with high levels of confusion)
    a.   Provide each person with a cup of silica sand, a container with a lid, and a selection of flowers.
    b.   Place one cup of sand in the bottom of the container.
    c.   Place flowers, face up, on top of sand layer keeping some space between each flower.
        * Gently pour more sand over flowers until all are completely covered.
    d.   Place lid on container.
    e.   Flowers will be ready for use in two to three weeks.

Preserving Flowers & Leaves

Helpful Hints

Concepts:
- Preserving plants.
- Projects that can be made from preserved plant materials.

Points of Interest:

Pressing
- Some flowers that press best are: purple cup flower, alyssum, celosia, geraniums, pansies, and wildflowers. (Always leave more wildflowers growing when you harvest and never take from a protected area.)
- When pressing a flower with a large center, do not press the entire flower, just remove the petals and press those. Some flowers in this category that press well are marigolds, zinnias, daisies, and mums.
- Most leaves press well. Some great leaves for fall color are oak, euonymous, crab apple, purple plum, red maple, and nandina.
- Flower presses can easily be made by taking two pieces of plywood cut to desired size, pieces of blotting paper (cut to a size a bit smaller than the wood) and rubber bands.
- A phone book with weight on it works great as a press, and phone books are always available, it seems.
- If you do not have two weeks, flowers can be pressed and placed in a microwave until dry. Look at books on pressed flower art for more details.

Preserving/Drying
- Silica sand is a bit expensive; however, it can be reused over and over.
- Flowers that work best with a single row of petals, such as a single marigold, or small tube flowers, such as mini-narcissus.

Adaptations:
✓ Individuals can help each other by partnering, e.g., one person prepares the flower petals and the other places the petals/greenery on the paper.

Notes

Sun Catchers

⏲ Time Allowed: 30 minutes

Goal Areas:
Fine Motor
Cognitive
Social/Emotional

Materials:

- Clear plastic adhesive shelf liner cut into 3-inch circles (need two per person)
- Hole punchers
- Thin colorful ribbon: one 12-inch piece and three 6-inch pieces for each person
- Pressed flowers
- Damp sponges or paper towels for each person
- Scissors
- Small garbage can for scraps

Precautions:
✓ Count scissors before, during and after the session.

Planning Notes:
✓ Flowers need to be pressed no less than 2 weeks in advance.
✓ Directions for pressing flowers on page 32.
✓ Have plastic circles cut in advance.
✓ Bend back a bit of the backing on each circle to lessen frustration if group has limited patience.

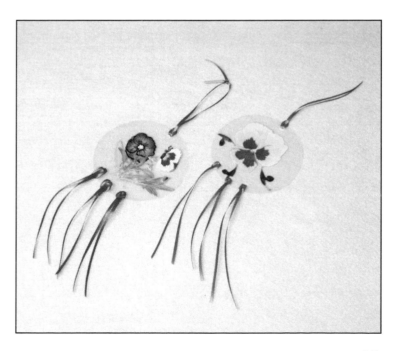

Sun Catchers

Step-by-Step Directions

1. Show an example of the finished project, discussing:
    * The concept of a sun catcher.
    * The pressed flower/reminisce process about planting, harvesting and pressing (if grown by participants).
2. Pull backing off of one of the clear plastic circles and lay it on the table, sticky side up.
3. Provide participants with a selection of pressed flowers.
4. Place flowers on the sticky plastic circle by:
    a. Wetting a finger with damp sponge or towel.
    b. Placing damp finger lightly on the desired flower and gently lifting the flower.
    c. Placing the flower on the plastic circle.
       (warning: once on the plastic, the flowers cannot be moved).
5. Continue this step until satisfied with the design.
6. Remove the backing from a second circle.
7. Lay the plastic circle (sticky side down) over the circle with flowers, matching edges as closely as possible.
8. Trim any uneven edges.
9. Using a hole punch, create holes for ribbon:
    a. One hole in top.
    b. Three holes in bottom.
10. Loop ribbon through top hole, tying to create a hanger.
11. Loop ribbons through bottom holes and let loose ends hang down for decoration. Trim, if needed.
12. Discuss how the sun catchers may be hung in a sunny window or gifted to a friend.

Sun Catchers

Helpful Hints

Concepts:

- Sun catchers.
- Process of pressing flowers.

Points of Interest:

- The Southwest Native Americans are thought to be the first to create sun catchers.
- The art of pressed flowers dates back to Victorian times.

Adaptations:

✓ To extend the session to a full hour, pick and press more flowers for future use. If you do not have a group garden, flowers can be picked ahead of time somewhere else and kept in a sealed plastic bag in the refrigerator for up to 2 days.

✓ See the activity, *Preserving Flowers and Leaves*, page 31.

✓ Use fall leaves instead of flowers and gold/orange ribbon for an autumn project.

✓ For a bit more money, clear laminating plastic can be used for a slightly nicer look.

✓ For a more elegant look, flowers can be placed between two pieces of beveled glass, sealing the glass edges with copper tape found at stained glass supply stores. This project would only be for those with high levels of fine motor skills.

✓ The completed sun catchers could be collected and used in creating a mobile.

Notes

Perky Pumpkins

⏱ **Time Allowed:** 45 minutes

Goal Areas:
Sensory
Fine Motor
Cognitive
Social/Emotional

Materials:
- Sample of project
- Waxed paper
- Mini-pumpkins (one per person)
- Small plates with craft glue and spreaders for each person.
- Craft eyes
- Small pompoms
- Small colorful craft feathers
- Strawflowers or artificial flowers
- Water-proof colored markers
- Wet paper towels for sticky fingers

Planning Notes:
- ✓ Make sample a day ahead.
- ✓ Look at Helpful Hints for adaptation suggestions.
- ✓ Mini pumpkins can be found in most grocery stores in the Autumn.
- ✓ This project could be a community service project by gifting finished pieces to children (age 5 and over) in hospitals, etc.

Precautions:
- ✓ If using decoupage, use only a non-toxic brand and place in something other than a cup or bowl to avoid being mistaken for a food or drink.

39

Perky Pumpkins

Step-by-Step Directions

1. At the beginning of the session, discuss the season and what comes to mind, e.g., fall leaves, chrysanthemums, pumpkins, etc.
2. Show a completed project to group.
3. Distribute to each person:
    * A placemat-size piece of waxed paper.
    * One pumpkin.
    * Glue plate and spreader.
4. Have everyone glue eyes on pumpkin by placing glue where the eyes are to go and then placing eyes on glue.
5. Have each person select a colored fuzzy ball for a nose.
6. Attach noses with glue in the same way the eyes were attached.
7. Draw a mouth on the pumpkin using colored water-proof markers.
8. Apply a layer of glue around the pumpkin's stem.
9. Place feather quills into glue.
10. Add glue to bottoms of artificial flowers or strawflowers.
11. Place glued flowers atop the feathers around stem.
12. Show off creations when complete and share what can be done with the creation.

Perky Pumpkins

Helpful Hints

Concepts:

* Seasons.

Points of Interest:

* This is a great project for reminiscing. Items for discussion could be:
  * Who has carved Jack-O-Lanterns?
  * Who has grown pumpkins in the past?
  * What are all the things that can be done with a pumpkin?
  * In what fairy tale does a pumpkin play a role?
  * In what season are we? Or, of what season do pumpkins remind you?
  * What flowers do you think of when you think of fall?
* Suggested pumpkins are 'Jack Be Little.'
* The pumpkin will last about one or two months before going mushy.

Adaptations:

* ✓ For a shinier, more "store-bought" look, the pumpkins can be painted with decoupage and allowed to dry before decorating.
* ✓ Those who desire, or with very good eye-hand coordination, could paint faces on the pumpkins using acrylic paints.
* ✓ If the budget allows, a small glue bottle for each person could be easier to use than glue on a plate with a spreader.
* ✓ To add another long-term element to the project, 'Jack Be Little' pumpkins could be grown in the summer garden.

Notes

Fall Leaf Window Art

⏱ Time Allowed: 45 minutes

Goal Areas:
Sensory
Fine Motor
Cognitive
Language
Social/Emotional

Materials:
- Sample of project
- Selection of pressed leaves (see page 32 for instructions on how to press flowers/leaves)
- One sheet of paper per person (8½ x 11)
- Plastic wrap, cut-to-fit sheets of paper
- Ribbon
- Iron
- Ironing board or suitable surface
- Dish towel
- Hole punch
- Scissors

Precautions:
✓ Provide one-on-one supervision with use of the hot iron.

Planning Notes:
✓ Press leaves at least two weeks in advance.
✓ Create a sample prior to session.
✓ Cut ribbon and plastic wrap in advance.
✓ Use a DRY iron. Steam will discolor the leaves.
✓ Do not use fresh leaves. They will become discolored in a few days.

43

Fall Leaf Window Art

Step-by-Step Directions

1. Open session with a discussion of the current season. Show samples of pressed leaves, describing how they were pressed to keep their color. After discussion, show a sample of what will be made during the session.

2. Provide each person with an 8½ x 11-inch sheet of white paper covered with a flat piece of plastic wrap. The paper is to assist with visually identifying the borders of the plastic.

3. Have each person select a handful of pressed leaves. Instruct participants to place the leaves on the sheet of plastic in any design they desire.

4. When all the leaves are in place, provide each person with another sheet of plastic. Have them lay it directly over the other piece and the leaves.

5. Have those who are able take turns at the ironing board or table.

6. With supervision, completely cover all of the plastic with a towel and then press with the hot, dry iron.

7. When completely sealed:
   a. Stop ironing.
   b. Remove towel.
   c. Punch a hole in top of the plastic.
   d. String a ribbon through the hole and tie in a knot to create a hanger.

8. When completed these are beautiful hanging in a window.

Fall Leaf Window Art

Helpful Hints

Vocabulary:
- Names of trees.
- Verbalize colors.

Concepts:
- Process of pressing leaves/flowers to preserve.
- Identifying the season.
- Process of leaves turning color in the fall.
- Process of melting with heat.

Points of Interest:
- Botanists throughout history have pressed flowers and leaves as a means of identifying plant materials.
- Many a grandmother has pressed flowers in a bible, especially those from weddings and christenings.
- Information on leaves changing color may easily be found on the internet.

Adaptations:
- ✓ For a more finished look, the completed pieces may be framed with a purchased or self-made mat.
- ✓ A similar activity can be done using waxed paper (instead of plastic wrap) and adding crayon shavings as well as the leaves. This is actually the more traditional method.

Notes

Holiday Sachets

🕐 **Time Allowed:** 45 minutes

Goal Areas:
Sensory
Fine Motor
Cognitive
Social/Emotional

Materials:
- Sample of project
- Cinnamon sticks
- Cloves
- Dried lemon peel
- Dried orange peel
- Small bowls (one per person)
- Sachet bags (one per person)
- Plastic spoons (one per person)
- Sprigs of artificial greenery
- Colored ribbon cut in 12-inch lengths

Precautions:
✓ Check with nursing regarding breathing issues.
✓ For those with severe cognitive challenges, use scoops instead of spoons.

Planning Notes:
✓ Create a sample prior to session.
✓ One or two weeks prior to sachet activity, incorporate discussion on citrus. Provide each person with a mandarin orange, encouraging them to peel and eat it. When done eating, have participants tear the peeling into small pieces and place in a cup to dry.

Holiday Sachets

Step-by-Step Directions

1. Begin by showing a finished sachet and passing it around for all to smell (facilitate this to help prevent contamination). Explain to the group how all the items in the potpourri mixture can be found at the grocery store.
   * These items were probably in their mother's and grandmother's pantries.
   * Discuss how a sachet might be used.
2. Provide each person with a small bowl.
3. Give each person a cinnamon stick.
4. Break cinnamon sticks into small pieces, placing pieces into bowl.
5. Encourage smelling the spice and then discuss cinnamon facts (see Helpful Hints on next page).
6. Continue Step 2 with:
   * Citrus peel.
   * Cloves (don't break).
7. Stir ingredients in bowl with spoon.
8. Fill sachet bags with mixture (see Adaptations on next page).
9. When the bag is full, pull the strings tight and tie into a knot (see Helpful Hints on next page for adaptations for those with use of only one hand).
10. Lay a piece of artificial greenery over the pulled strings and tie on with piece of colored ribbon.
11. When complete, provide the opportunity for each person to share whether he/she will keep the sachet or give it away.

Holiday Sachets

Helpful Hints

Vocabulary:
- Cinnamon
- Cloves
- Spices

Concepts:
- Potpourri: A mixture of fragrant natural items to scent a room.
- Sachets: Used to scent linen closets, dresser drawers, closets. Some for fragrance only, others are used to repel insects.

Points of Interest:
- Spices: Where do they come from? Indonesia, primarily.
- Cinnamon is actually bark from a tree.
- Cloves are actually dried flower buds.
- Citrus trees are originally from Asia.

Adaptations:
- ✓ For individuals with the use of only one hand, partner them with a neighboring participant. Have one person hold the bag while the other spoons in the ingredients.
- ✓ Another method for those with use of only one hand, or with coordination issues, is to place the sachet bag in a small cup and tape the cup to the table.
- ✓ For individuals with high levels of confusion, use small scoops instead of spoons and boxes or bags instead of dishes. This will assist in lessening the tendency to ingest the project materials.
- ✓ For those with limited fine motor skills, wired ribbon can be easily twisted around the top of the bag for decoration.

Notes

Activity Plans

PLANTING PROJECTS

Notes

Mini Terrariums

⏰ **Time Allowed:** 60 minutes

Goal Areas:
Fine Motor
Upper Gross Motor
Cognitive
Social/Emotional

Materials:

- Sample of project
- Clear plastic containers with lids
- Aquarium gravel
- Aquarium charcoal
- Suitable plants (Swedish ivy, fittonia, peperomia, ferns)
- Potting mix in re-sealable plastic bags
- Scoops
- Pens/pencils
- Scissors
- Warm water
- Room-temperature water

Planning Notes:

✓ Create sample in advance of session.
✓ Collect containers in advance.

Precautions:

✓ Closely supervise the use of the gravel, charcoal and soil to prevent anyone ingesting materials.
  Always place items such as gravel in containers that are not associated with eating or drinking.

Mini Terrariums

Step-by-Step Directions

1. Initiate discussion about terrariums by:
   * Showing pictures.
   * Showing an actual terrarium.
   * Share some history of terrariums and how the cycles take place within a closed garden (from next page Points of Interest).
2. Distribute terrarium containers and have participants follow instructions:
   a. Cover bottom of terrarium with at least ½-inch of gravel.
   b. Add a thin layer of charcoal to just cover the gravel.
   c. Set aside while doing Step 3.
3. Moisten potting mix with warm water in a re-sealable plastic bag until evenly dark in color but not drippy.
4. Return terrarium container and:
   a. Cover gravel and charcoal with a 2-inch layer of potting mix, pressed in firmly.
   b. Determine where plants are to go and make a hole for each.
   c. Place cuttings in holes and firm potting mix around stems.
   d. Sprinkle colored gravel around plants for decoration. Water gently around each plant using room temperature water.
5. Clean inside walls of container by pouring a tiny amount of water down walls or wipe with tissue.
6. Put on lid and place the terrarium in indirect light.
7. Visit about how to provide proper care.
8. By keeping the lid on, there will be no need to water unless the soil becomes light colored.

Mini Terrariums

Helpful Hints

Concepts:

- Size: tall, short, small, and large.
- Shape: round, cube, cylinder, octagon, etc.
- Water Cycle: evaporation, condensation, precipitation. Good information and charts that show this cycle relating to the water cycle on this planet can be found on the internet.

Points of Interest:

- Terrariums were first used by early discoverers as a way of keeping plants alive when bringing them back to their homelands from far across the oceans. Sea water could not be used and drinking water needed to be saved for the crew.
- Moisture from the soil and plants evaporates and rises to the surface. Then it condenses and returns to the soil like rain and the cycle continues.
- As long as the seal is tight, there is no need to add water in the future.
- Charcoal keeps the terrarium water "sweet." Did you know that charcoal is often used in water filters to create better-tasting water?
- What makes a good terrarium container? Anything clear that can be sealed. Aquarium tanks, canning jars, soda bottles, giant pickle jars, giant water bottles, etc., all would be suitable.
- Terrariums need to be kept out of direct light as plants can be burned from the intensity of the sun through the clear glass or plastic.

Adaptations:

- ✓ To encourage more socialization and cooperation among peers you can develop teams and have each team cooperatively create a terrarium.
- ✓ The project is most easily done using a container with an opening large enough to easily fit a hand through.
- ✓ Ice cream sundae dishes with tops from fast-food restaurants make great mini terrariums.

Notes

Root Race!

⏲ **Time Allowed:** 45 minutes

Goal Areas:
Sensory
Fine Motor
Gross Motor
Cognitive
Social/Emotional

Materials:
- Four foam cups
- Pencils
- Potting mix
- Peat moss
- Perlite
- Vermiculite
- Water-proof markers
- Bottles of warm water
- Four saucers
- Cuttings from one type of plant
- Seven gallon-size re-sealable plastic bags
- Drinking straws
- Aprons
- Disposable, non-latex gloves

Precautions:
✓ Avoid creating dust with the perlite and the vermiculite.
✓ Carefully observe to prevent anyone ingesting the materials.
✓ Assist where necessary with washing materials off hands.

Planning Notes:
✓ Select only one type of plant to use. If using ficus, take the cuttings 15 minutes in advance of session to let milky sap dry.
✓ Place potting mix, peat moss and perlite in separate re-sealable bags and moisten in advance of session.
✓ Seat participants at the table with people they will team well with.
✓ If including anyone with cognitive impairments, monitor closely to prevent anyone ingesting the mediums.

Root Race!

Step-by-Step Directions

1. Discuss with group that they will be working in teams and performing an experiment to see which growing medium is the easiest for plants to root. The plants will be checked weekly to see which one roots first.

2. Show the plant that will be used and make cuttings. Encourage group to reminisce regarding plants they may have started from cuttings or "slips."

3. Divide the group into four teams and provide all with aprons and gloves, assisting anyone needing help.

   * Procedure for perlite, peat moss & potting mix teams:
       a. Punch three small holes in bottom of cup.
       b. Using water-proof marker, write date and names of team on cup.
       c. Mix warm water into a bag of selected medium.
       d. Fill cup with moist medium.
       e. Make one hole in center of medium about 1½-inch deep.
       f. Place cutting in the hole.
       g. Gently press medium around the cutting stem.
       h. Water cutting generously and let drain in a tray.
       i. When adequately drained, place in a re-sealable bag.
       j. Seal bag leaving room to insert straw at one end.
       k. Insert straw and blow on straw until the bag is inflated. Remove the straw and seal the bag.
       l. Place completed project under lights or near a sunny window.
       m. Once a week, check for rooting by very gently pulling on cutting. If it resists your pull, it has started rooting. It is best to provide supervision for this test.

Step-by-Step Directions Continued

* <u>Procedure for vermiculite team:</u>

a. Punch three small holes in bottom of cup.

b. Using water-proof marker, write date and names of team on cup.

c. Fill cup with dry vermiculite.

d. Place cup in a saucer and dampen with warm water.

e. Make one hole in center of medium about 1½-inch deep.

f. Place cutting in the hole.

g. Gently press medium around the cutting stem.

h. Water cutting generously and let drain in a tray.

i. When adequately drained, place in a re-sealable bag.

j. Seal bag leaving room to insert straw at one end.

k. Insert straw and blow on straw until the bag is inflated. Remove the straw and seal the bag.

l. Place completed project under lights or near a sunny window.

m. Once a week, check for rooting by very gently pulling on cutting. If it resists your pull, it has started rooting. It is best to provide supervision for this test.

Root Race!

Helpful Hints

Concepts:
- Propagation techniques.
- Plant parts.

Points of Interest:
- It is necessary to use the same plant for each cutting to create the "constant" in this experiment, e.g., if you were to use coleus for some and hibiscus for others, the coleus would naturally root faster no matter which medium it was in.
- Plants that work great for this experiment are: ficus benjamina (weeping fig), plectranthus australis (Swedish ivy) and peperomia obtusifolia.
- Sometimes plants will develop a cluster of cells called a "callus" at the base of the cut stem prior to sending out roots.
- If the cutting pulls out of the vermiculite or perlite easily while checking for rooting, look for this callus before placing back in the medium.
- The horticultural term for rooting cuttings is "stem propagation."
- This project uses a form of stem propagation called a "tip cutting."

Adaptations:
- ✓ One other rooting medium could be a cube of floral foam. Be sure to use the type meant for fresh flower use. Cut a piece of foam, place it in a cup (no holes), soak the foam with water, then stick in the cutting. When finished, place the cup in a re-sealable bag and fill with air as done with the previous directions. Poinsettias and chrysanthemums are propagated in this type of foam in commercial greenhouses.
- ✓ Consider keeping a written or photo journal that describes the "root race" in detail.

Stems and Stones

⏰ **Time Allowed:** 45 minutes

Goal Areas:
Sensory
Fine Motor
Cognitive
Social/Emotional

Materials:

- Sample of project
- One clear plastic cup (party-size or bigger) per person
- Four 4-oz. cups per person to hold gravel and water
- Three colors of aquarium gravel (located in pet supply section of stores)
- Two to three small rooted cuttings per person
- Water-proof markers and masking tape
- Water-soluble fertilizer
- Water bottles or cans filled with diluted fertilizer solution

Precautions:

✓ This project is not appropriate for use with either the very young or individuals with severe cognitive impairment due to the potential for ingesting the gravel and/or the fertilizer mixture.

Planning Notes:

✓ Create a sample prior to start of session
✓ Propagate cuttings of plants in water 2 weeks prior to session.
✓ Prior to start of session, pour colored gravels into small cups so that each person will have one cup of each color gravel.
✓ Mix 1/4 tsp. water-soluble fertilizer/gallon of water and pour into water bottles or water cans.

Stems and Stones

Step-by-Step Directions

1. Show a completed project to group and discuss the concept of growing in water (see Helpful Hints on next page).
2. Hand out clear plastic cups.
3. Place masking tape to side of cup.
4. Write name on the tape using a water-proof marker.
5. Distribute cup of blue gravel per person.
6. Demonstrate pouring gravel into clear cup and have participants do the same.
7. Demonstrate placing plants into cup allowing them to rest against the side of the cup. Point out that the plant just rests on the surface of the gravel, no holes are needed.
8. Have participants do the same.
9. Gently pour a different color of gravel around the plants.
10. Top off with the remaining color of gravel.
11. Fill planted container three-quarters full with diluted fertilizer solution.
12. Instruct participants to keep the planters:
    * Filled with water.
    * Near a sunny window.

Stems and Stones

Helpful Hints

Concepts:
- The science of hydroponics.

Points of Interest:
- Great plants for this project are spider plant, inch plant (or spiderwort), Swedish ivy, begonia, and impatiens. The spider plant is also known as the friendship plant or the airplane plant.
- If working with older adults, consider asking if anyone remembers starting a slip of a plant for a friend.
- Soil is not required to grow plants. The science of growing plants in just water and nutrients is called hydroponics. Many greenhouse tomatoes are raised hydroponically.

Adaptations:
- ✓ Larger water gardens can be made using any clear plastic container, even empty peanut butter jars.
- ✓ Un-rooted cuttings can be used if you do not have the space to prepare in advance.

Notes

Sense-Sational Succulents

🕐 **Time Allowed:** 60 minutes

Goal Areas:
Sensory
Fine Motor
Cognitive
Language
Social/Emotional

Materials:

- "Mother" plants: recommended are haworthias, echeverias
- Mini-loaf aluminum pans (punch drainage holes in bottom) or 4-inch pots
- Re-sealable plastic bags filled with cactus potting mix, moistened with hot tap water
- Scoops
- Plastic labels
- Water-proof markers
- Small cups
- Water bottles filled with lukewarm water
- Trays for watering

Planning Notes:

✓ Purchase succulents. Look for pots with many "pups" around the "mother" plant.
✓ Prepare drainage holes in pans in advance.
✓ Fill bags with two mini loaf pans of potting mix each prior to start of session.
✓ Add approximately 4 ounces of warm water to soil just prior to start of session and re-seal bags eliminating as much air in bag as possible before sealing.

Sense-Sational Succulents

Step-by-Step Directions

1. As the session starts, show the mother plants and discuss the concept of *division* (see Helpful Hints on next page). When the new plants from today have rooted, they will be used in dish gardens.
2. Invite group to join in verbalizing the names of the plants and the word "succulent."
3. Have teams of two work warm water into a bag of cactus mix, kneading the bag until the mix is evenly moist (not too wet).
4. Have each team fill a loaf pan or pot with cactus mix to within ½-inch of the pan top.
5. Have teams plant the pups in the pans/pots of mix.
6. Label each pan/pot with the date and names of those who did the planting.
7. Place planted pans/pots in a tray.
8. Water each with half of a 4-ounce cup.
9. Place the tray of planted pans/pots under proper light (see Helpful Hints on next page).
10. Water twice a week.

Sense-Sational Succulents

Helpful Hints

Vocabulary:

- "S" sounds.
- Names of succulents.

Concepts:

- All cacti are succulents, but not all succulents are cacti.
- Ways plants adapt to their environment.
- Propagation techniques.

Points of Interest:

- Many plants reproduce not only through seed, but also through division of what are called "off-sets" or pups.
- The original plant is often called the mother plant.
- The off-sets may be gently pulled away from the mother plant and planted separately.
- Some plants that produce off-sets are:
  * Haworthias
  * Aloes
  * Echeverias
  * African violets
- What are succulents?
  * Plants whose stems, and sometimes leaves, are filled with liquid, helping them to survive in dry climates.
- Care of succulents
  * Water only when soil is dry.
  * Keep in sunny window or under artificial lighting.

Notes

Sense-Sational Succulents 2

⏱ Time Allowed: 60 minutes

Goal Areas:
Sensory
Fine Motor
Gross Motor
Language
Social/Emotional

Materials:
- Sample of project
- Dishes deep enough for plant roots
- Cactus mix in trays, moistened with warm water
- One 4-oz. cup/scoop of clean gravel per person
- One-half of a 4-oz. cup/scoop of aquarium charcoal per person
- Three succulent plants per person
- Appropriate decorations (see Helpful Hints on page 71 for more explanation)
- Masking tape
- Water-proof markers
- Disposable, non-latex gloves

Precautions:
✓ Either delete final decorative additions or find appropriately safe decorations if doing project with those who have a high level of confusion or are very young.
✓ Use scoops when working with those with high cognitive impairment or very young.

Planning Notes:
✓ Use the succulents grown at least a month earlier in the Sense-Sational Succulents project (page 65) or purchase plants.
✓ Make a sample earlier.
✓ Get warm water just before the start of session.
✓ Place gravel and charcoal in 4-oz. cups/scoops in advance.

Sense-Sational Succulents 2

Step-by-Step Directions

1. Show a sample of the project.
2. If the plants were propagated earlier by the group, reminisce regarding how and when they were started.
3. Pass plants around for all to feel, noting the differences.
4. Provide each person with an empty planter, containers of gravel and charcoal.
   a. Place cup/scoop of gravel in bottom of planter, spread evenly, explaining this provides drainage.
   b. Sprinkle charcoal over gravel, explaining this acts as a water filter and keeps the drainage water from smelling.
5. Pass out trays of cactus mix with warm water added.
6. Have participants put on gloves
   a. Stir mixture until evenly dark in color.
   b. Cover gravel and charcoal with a thin layer of cactus mix.
7. Remove plants from pots, set in bowl in desired positions. You may need to spread out the roots.
8. Fill container with cactus mix, firming soil around plant roots. Fill to within ¼-inch of planter top.
9. Decorate as desired and as appropriate for cognitive levels.
10. Do not water on planting day, but distribute instructions to dampen with 2 Tbsp. of water the following day.
11. Instruct to place planter in indirect sunlight and water when soil is dry.
12. Have discussion regarding water needs of succulents.

Helpful Hints

Concepts:

- Desert plant characteristics and care.

Points of Interest:

- Ideally, select plants with different textures. Great plants for this project are:
  * Jade plant: Plump, rubbery leaves that are cool to the touch.
  * Haworthia: There are many of these, but the common names of two good choices are:
    * Window pane plant: Translucent leaves. This allows the plant to absorb as much sunshine as possible to make food when it is covered with sand.
    * Zebra or pearl plant: White bumps in stripes, excellent for tactile stimulation.
  * Aloe vera: A common plant, the juice is good for burns.
  * Panda plant: An excellent plant for tactile stimulation due to its fuzzy leaves.
- Succulents are plants that have fleshy stems and/or leaves. They need much less water than tropical foliage plants.

Adaptations:

- ✓ How to save money and create extra projects:
  * When purchasing plants, look for pots of haworthia that contain many little plants. You can save money by dividing those plants … you may get eight plants out of one pot.
  * Four-inch pots of jade and panda with three plants per pot.
  * Jade plants & panda plants can be started easily as cuttings.
  * Pots or saucers could be painted in a separate session.

Notes

Plants From Seeds

🕐 **Time Allowed:** 60 minutes

Goal Areas:
Sensory
Fine Motor
Cognitive
Language
Social/Emotional

Materials:

- Pictures of plants to be grown, or actual plants
- Mini-loaf aluminum pans (punch drainage holes in bottom)
- Quart-size re-closable plastic bags filled with seed-starting mix and moistened with hot tap water
- Seed (mixed with 2 Tbsp. sand per package of seed if the seed is tiny)
- One small bag of vermiculite
- 4-oz. cups or scoops
- Plastic labels
- Water-proof markers
- Empty trays for watering
- Sponges
- Bowl of warm water
- Disposable, non-latex gloves
- Aprons (optional)

Precautions:

✓ Use scoops when working with those with high cognitive impairment or very young.

Planning Notes:

✓ Cut out pictures of the plants to be grown from seed catalogues or magazines.
✓ Punch holes in loaf pans prior to start of session.
✓ Choose plants from the Helpful Hints page to start.

Plants From Seeds

Step-by-Step Directions

1.   Explaining the project: to propagate (start) plants from seed.
2.   Show either a grown plant or pictures of the plant. Ask if anyone has grown this type of plant before (see information in Helpful Hints on next page).
3.   Break group into teams of two.
4.   Have teams work warm water into bag of potting mix until evenly dark and moist, not drippy.
5.   Have each team fill a loaf pan with potting mix to within ½-inch of top using a small scoop to fill.
6.   Place seeds on soil surface (about 10 seeds per pan or sprinkle mixture of seed and sand on the soil surface).
7.   Cover seeds with vermiculite until all soil is hidden.
8.   Place the seed pan in a bin or tray and have team members take turns soaking sponges in bowl of water and then squeezing them over the seed pans.
9.   Continue until water starts dripping from the bottom of the planter.
10. Write participant names and date on one side of label and write the plant name on the other side. Place label in one end of the planter.
11. Place tray of seeded pans under proper light (see Helpful Hints on next page).
12. Water at least twice a week using the sponge method.

Plants From Seeds

Helpful Hints

Concepts:
- Propagating from seed (sexual propagation).
- Stages of growth from seed to plant.

Points of Interest:
- Most books will suggest covering the seeds with soil mix, but by covering with vermiculite, you can cut your watering during the week in half.
- Seeding in mini-loaf pans found in any supermarket is an easy way for everyone to plant without having too many plants for a small space.
- Light and warmth are necessary for good growth. Ideally, place no more than 12 inches below fluorescent or "grow" lights, or place in a windowsill if the weather is warm.
- Most bedding plant seedlings want to grow in cool temperatures.
- If temperatures are too warm, plants will tend to get "leggy."
- Those plants listed below do well in warmer indoor temperatures:
  - * Marigolds
  - * Geraniums
  - * Peppers
  - * Tomatoes
  - * Basil
  - * Zinnias
  - * Celosia
  - * Coleus
  - * Statice
  - * Strawflowers

Adaptations:
- ✓ When seeding any of the above, be sure to check on package to determine correct timing for starting indoors.
- ✓ To extend the lesson, you could include posters showing stages of plant growth or, for young children, coloring pages showing the stages.
- ✓ To aid in picking up seeds more easily, have participants wet a finger using a damp sponge, press the damp finger to a seed, and then flick seed off of finger and onto soil in the pan.

Notes

Transplanting Seedlings

⏱ **Time Allowed:** 60 minutes

Goal Areas:
Sensory
Fine Motor
Gross Motor
Cognitive
Social/Emotional

Materials:
- Seedlings
- Sterilized nursery cell packs
- Trays filled with potting mix
- Hot water in water cans
- Disposable, non-latex gloves
- Plastic forks
- Water-proof markers
- Blank labels
- Water bottles filled with lukewarm water
- Empty trays without holes for watering

Planning Notes:
✓ Sterilize the plastic cell packs by washing and rinsing prior to start. This could be incorporated in a previous project.
✓ Prepare hot water shortly before starting.
✓ Have trays of seedlings that were started a few weeks ago on hand.

Transplanting Seedlings

Step-by-Step Directions

1. At start of session, explain that the project is to transplant seedlings started a few weeks ago.
2. Show the young plants to all.
3. Divide the group into teams of two and have each team:
    a. Work warm water into potting mix until evenly moist.
    b. Fill one cell pack with potting mix to within ½-inch of top, being careful not to pack tightly.
4. Using a pen or dowel, make one hole in the center of each cell's soil.
5. (Staff when appropriate) Using fork, gently lift seedlings out of trays.
6. Instruct on how to hold seedling: hold by leaves, not stem.
7. Give each team six seedlings and have them plant one seedling in each hole so that soil is up to first set of leaves. Gently firm soil around each seedling.
8. Add the date to old label or make a new label with plant name, date, etc.
9. Place label in one end of the planter.
10. Place cell pack in tray and water gently until water drains from bottom.
11. After draining, place the cell packs in dry trays.
12. Place the tray(s) of transplanted seedlings under proper light (see Helpful Hints on next page).
13. Water at least three times a week.

Transplanting Seedlings

Helpful Hints

Concepts:
- Stages of growth from seed to plant.

Points of Interest:
- The best time to transplant is when the first set of "true leaves" appear. These are actually the second set of leaves to appear. The first leaves that show are called the cotyledons.
- Sometimes seedlings are still too small to handle even though their true leaves are out. Coleus are like this. Wait to transplant until the seedlings can be easily handled.
- The process of lifting the seedlings out of the seed bed is called "pricking off."
- Light is necessary for good growth. Ideally, place plants no more than 12 inches from fluorescent lights, or "grow" lights, or place in a windowsill if weather is warm.
- Always be sure that the cell packs are clean. They should be thoroughly washed with soapy water and rinsed before use to avoid disease problems.
- In a month or two, plants may be planted outdoors, if there is no chance of frost, or moved into pots to be grown as houseplants indoors.

Adaptations:
- ✓ To help keep the soil around the plants moist, line trays with either capillary matting (purchased from specialty horticultural catalogues) or cut up disposable diapers. By keeping this lining wet, the soil in the cell packs will absorb water from below without giving the plants root rot. This practice can cut down on the frequency of watering.
- ✓ To further the lesson, you could include posters showing stages of plant growth or, for young children, coloring pages showing the stages.

Notes

Sensational Sunflowers

⏱ Time Allowed: 45 minutes

Goal Areas:
Sensory
Fine Motor
Gross Motor
Language
Social/Emotional

Materials:
- Pictures of sunflowers
- Hulled edible sunflower seeds
- One 16-oz. plastic cup per person
- Clean stones or gravel in 3- to 4-oz. cups/scoops
- Sunflower-design sticky shelf paper with flowers cut out
- Disposable, non-latex gloves
- Aprons (optional)
- Potting mix in trays with warm water added
- Water-proof markers
- Poem cards (see Planning Notes)
- 'Teddy Bear' or other mini-sunflower seeds
- Warm water in bottles or 3-oz. cups

Precautions:
✓ Observe cognitively impaired and/or very young participants closely to prevent ingesting of materials.

Planning Notes:
✓ Prepare a copy of this poem for each person prior to session:

> This seed won't change much in the next minute or hour… but with time, light and water it becomes
> A sunflower!!!!!!

✓ Prep soil and gravel prior to start of session.
✓ Dwarf sunflower seeds can be found at specialty nurseries or purchased mail order.

Sensational Sunflowers

Step-by-Step Directions

1. Open the session by showing pictures of sunflowers and, *if appropriate for group,* distribute edible sunflower seeds to nibble on. Explain that the session's project is starting a miniature sunflower from seed.
2. Distribute one plastic cup per person.
3. Have everyone write his/her name on the bottom of the cup.
4. Provide each person with some sticky backed sunflower pictures and:
    a. Peel backing off sunflower pictures.
    b. Adhere pictures to outside of cup.
5. Place a scoop of clean gravel or rocks in the bottom of each cup to provide drainage.
6. Put on gloves for soil mixing.
7. Working in teams of two, mix warm water into potting mix until evenly dark.
8. Fill the decorated cup almost to the top with moistened potting mix.
9. Using a pointer finger or a pencil, make three holes (½-inch deep) near the center of cup.
10. Place one seed in each hole and cover with mix.
11. Water planters until damp but not soggy (¼-cup).
12. Attach poem card (see Planning Notes on previous page).
13. Once seeds have germinated, cut off the weakest seedlings, leaving one strong plant.

Sensational Sunflowers

Helpful Hints

Concepts:

- How seeds grow: pictures or posters can be used that show how a seed sprouts, showing the cotyledon and roots.

Points of Interest:

- Sunflower facts:
  - ✳ The Sunflower State is Kansas.
  - ✳ Sunflower seeds are very good for our health.
  - ✳ Sunflowers get their name in part because they follow the sun with their "faces."
  - ✳ Sunflower seeds are a favorite of many birds.

Adaptations:

- ✓ Regular pots could be used instead of plastic cups. In this case, no gravel is needed for drainage.
- ✓ If unable to locate the sunflower sticky shelf paper, pictures of sunflowers can be cut from seed catalogues and pasted to the cup with decoupage during a prior session.
- ✓ When working with cognitively impaired and/or the very young, use scoops instead of cups to hold the gravel.

Notes

Mixing It Up

⏱ *Time Allowed:* 30 minutes

Goal Areas:
Sensory
Upper Gross Motor
Social/Emotional

Materials:
- Aprons
- One gallon-size re-sealable plastic bag per person
- Scoops
- Quart bags of:
  - Peat moss
  - Vermiculite
  - Moistened Perlite
- Bottles of hot tap water

Precautions:
✓ Moisten the perlite prior to session to avoid issues with dust.

Planning Notes:
✓ Purchase high-quality re-sealable bags to ensure good seals.
✓ Fill the bottles of hot water just before the start of the session to ensure the correct temperature.
✓ Avoid purchasing the lowest priced peat moss, as it is often poor quality.

Mixing It Up

Step-by-Step Directions

1. Start with an explanation of the project and why it is being done (*for a planting project the same day or another day, for a sale, etc.*)
2. Distribute one gallon-size re-sealable bag to each person.
3. Introduce peat moss (see Helpful Hints on next page).
4. Invite each person to place three scoops of peat moss into his/her bag.
5. Introduce vermiculite (see Helpful Hints on next page) and have each person place three scoops of vermiculite into his/her bag.
6. Introduce perlite (see Helpful Hints on next page) and have each person place one scoop of <u>dampened</u> perlite into his/her bag.
7. Pour ½ cup warm tap water into each bag.
8. Squeeze the air out of the bags and seal their tops, double checking to be sure the bag is completely closed.
9. Instruct participants to mix soil by gently kneading the bag until all the mix is evenly dark.
10. Check occasionally during mixing, adding more water if mix is still light colored. The mix should be damp but not dripping.
11. *If not using right away, skip Step 7 and have participants mix the dry ingredients only. Write names on bags and store for future use.*

Mixing It Up

Helpful Hints

Concepts:
- Surface tension.
- Growing mediums.

Points of Interest:
- Most potting mixes today are actually "soilless" mixes.
- All good potting mixes should be sterile to prevent insect and disease problems.
- Garden soil has three drawbacks when working with houseplants:
  * It is not sterile and the process to sterilize it is messy.
  * It becomes cement-like when placed in a pot.
  * This compaction does not allow for healthy root growth of containerized plants.
- Use warm-hot water when moistening peat-based mixes.
  * Peat moss is harvested from underground in peat bogs that have been created from decaying plant material over great periods of time. It is a non-renewable resource and horticulturists are working at developing alternatives. One alternative is being made with coconut hulls.
  * Vermiculite is the layered clay, mica, that has been mined and then heated to an extremely high temperature until it puffs up. Because of its layers, vermiculite is very absorbent which makes it excellent for a potting mix. In the past, vermiculite has been used as insulation, kitty litter, and for soaking up spills such as car oil.
  * Perlite is mined from volcanic rock. It also is heated to an extremely high temperature until it puffs up like popcorn. Like the volcanic rock that it is mined from, perlite is very porous. It allows for drainage and yet holds on to oxygen particles. Due to its volcanic nature, it produces a dust that should not be inhaled. Always dampen the perilite before working with it.

Notes

New From Old

🕐 **Time Allowed:** 60 minutes

Goal Areas:
Sensory
Fine Motor
Upper Gross Motor
Cognitive
Social/Emotional

Planning Notes:
✓ Take cuttings just prior to start of session.
✓ Purchase suitable, non-toxic plants.

Materials:
- Disposable, non-latex gloves
- Foam or paper cups
- Trays of damp potting mix
- Warm and cool water
- Water-proof markers and pencils
- Desired non-toxic plant(s)
- Gallon-size re-sealable plastic bags
- Drinking straws

Precautions:
✓ Have each person wear gloves to be in compliance with the instructions on the bags of potting mix. Double check on plant toxicity (Appendix I, page 160).

New From Old

Step-by-Step Directions

1. Show examples of the plants that the cuttings were taken from.
2. Engage participants in reminiscence of the plants. Depending on cognitive levels that might include where the plants had been grown, e.g., garden. With those who have a high level of cognitive impairment, just reminiscing regarding the type of plant and memories of their parents, and/or grandparents growing them would be more appropriate.
3. Distribute cups and pencils to each individual and instruct them on the following steps:
   a. Using the sharp pencil tip, poke three holes in the bottom of cup.
   b. With water-proof marker, write name, date and the name of the plant on the cup.
   c. Set cups aside until done with Step 4.
4. Wearing gloves, mix warm water into potting mix.
5. Fill cup with the potting mix.
6. Using a pencil, make one hole in the soil for each cutting.
7. Place one cutting in each hole.
8. Gently press the potting mix around the stems of each cutting.
9. Place cup of cuttings in a bin or tray and water generously, leaving in bin to drain.
10. When draining is complete, place two cups of cuttings in a re-sealable plastic bag.
11. Seal the bag, leaving a slight opening at one end. Insert straw in the opening and blow up the bag like a balloon.
12. Pull out the straw and seal the bag completely.
13. Place the bag of cuttings under lights or in a sunny window.
14. Explain the plants will need at least two weeks to form roots.

Helpful Hints

Concepts:

- Rooting.
- Transpiration.
- Respiration.
- Terrariums.

Points of Interest:

- The type of cuttings used in this project are called "tip" cuttings. It is a form of stem propagation. Another form of stem propagation is "mallet" cuttings. This cutting has a T-shape at the end that enters the soil. For some plants, this provides two spots for rooting.
- Nodes are the bumps where leaves come out. When under the soil, nodes produce roots instead of leaves. Some plants will root anywhere along the stem, but many will not. Always have at least one node of a cutting under ground to ensure rooting.
  - ✳ To test for rooting: After two weeks, open the bags and pull gently on plants. If they resist coming out of the soil, they have roots. If plants pull out easily, re-stick them in the soil and firm soil gently around stem, then re-seal the bag as before. When rooted, leave plants in open bag for at least 24 hours to acclimate to the drier air.
- Good plants for this project are coleus, Swedish ivy, and peperomia.

Adaptations:

- ✓ For individuals who have the use of only one arm, taping the cup to the table will help stabilize it while it is being filled with soil and planted.
- ✓ Those who are able to use scissors safely, could make the cuttings.

Notes

Planting Rooted Cuttings

⏱ **Time Allowed:** 60 minutes

Goal Areas:
Fine Motor
Upper Gross Motor
Cognitive
Language
Social/Emotional

Planning Notes:
✓ Open bags of cuttings at least 24 hours in advance of this session.

Materials:
- "Mother" plants
- Rooted cuttings
- Plastic cups (same size as decorated cups) with holes cut in bottom for drainage
- Disposable, non-latex gloves
- Potting mix in trays, moistened with hot water
- Scoops
- Pre-decorated cups (see page 19)
- Water bottles filled with warm water
- Bowl for emptying excess water

Precautions:
✓ Closely supervise the use of the soil to prevent anyone ingesting.

Planting Rooted Cuttings

Step-by-Step Directions

1. Show the mother plant (where the cuttings came from) and explain how the project for the day is to pot up the rooted cuttings propagated from this larger plant.
    *   Discuss the term "propagation" and/or "cuttings."
    *   Pass plant around for all to look at and touch.
    *   Share what date the cuttings were started and invite any reminiscing about that project.
2. Divide group into teams of two.
3. Put on gloves
4. Mix warm water into a tray of potting mix until evenly moist (not too wet).
5. Fill plain cups approximately half full with potting mix. This amount may vary depending on root size. Roots should be covered but the stem should not be buried.
6. Assist with taking rooted cuttings out of pots by tipping pot upside down and tapping.
7. Place rooted cutting in cup and fill the cup loosely with soil mix. Tap cup now and then to settle the soil.
8. Set plain cup with plant into decorated cup (from *Picture Perfect Pots* activity, page 19).
9. Water.
10. Pour out any excess water that collected in decorated cup.
11. Instruct participants in the following:
    *   Place the plant near a sunny window.
    *   Water when soil feels dry or pot is light weight.

Planting Rooted Cuttings

Helpful Hints

Vocabulary:

- Propagation.
- Peat moss.
- Perlite.
- Vermiculite.

Concepts:

- Stem propagation.
- Watering.

Points of Interest:

- Even though many plants will root in water, if propagated in soil the plant goes through less shock when being potted after rooting.
- Plants propagated in plastic bags need to acclimate for at least one day by remaining in the bag, but opening the top to allow air in.
- Early explorers would take cuttings of exotic plants back to their homeland. They would propagate in pots of soil and place glass jars over the top to hold in the moisture.

Adaptations:

- ✓ For a less messy process, place potting mix in a re-sealable plastic bag along with some hot water. Squeeze out as much air as possible and re-seal. Participants mix the soil by kneading the bag, much like one would knead bread dough.

Notes

Bulb Beauties

⏲ **Time Allowed:** 60 minutes

Planning Notes:
✓ When purchasing bulbs, select ones that are firm. Select amaryllis bulbs that have bloom stalk(s) just starting to show.

Materials:
- Two amaryllis bulbs
- Two 6- to 8-inch pots
- Two 6- to 8-inch saucers
- Five paper white narcissus bulbs
- Clear bowl or clear tall vase
- Trays filled with potting mix moistened with hot tap water
- Clean gravel
- Water-proof markers
- Labels
- Lukewarm water
- Empty trays for watering
- Pictures or live samples of blooming bulbs
- Disposable, non-latex gloves

Precautions:
✓ This project is not safe for those with severe cognitive impairment or the very young. Most bulbs are toxic, if eaten.
✓ If you choose to add hyacinth bulbs to the activity, know their papery hull causes a skin reaction.
   Always wear gloves and closely supervise anyone working with these bulbs.

Bulb Beauties

Step-by-Step Directions

1. Begin session by explaining the concept of "forcing bulbs." Show pictures of what the bulbs will grow to be or show living examples (see Helpful Hints on next page for discussion questions).

2. Divide into three teams (two amaryllis teams, one narcissus team).

3. Have the two Amaryllis Teams work warm water into potting mix until evenly moist. Fill pots half full of potting mix.

4. Have third team (Narcissus Team) fill their clear container one-third full with gravel. All teams place bulbs on surface of either soil or gravel. Do not push in or try to bury.

5. Cover bulbs to their necks with soil for amaryllis teams and gravel for narcissus team.

6. On labels write:
    * Names of team members.
    * Date.
    * Name of plant.

7. Place label inside pot next to edge.

8. Place amaryllis pots in tray and water gently until water drains from bottom.

9. Place watered pots in saucers.

10. Water narcissus until water can be seen at the bottom of the bulbs.

11. Place all bulbs in sunny, cool location and water twice a week.

Bulb Beauties

Helpful Hints

Concepts:
- Stages of growth from bulb to mature plant.
- Contents of a bulb: The idea that the entire plant is already in the bulb.
- Recognition that outer appearances can be deceiving: Bulb is ugly on the outside but contains great beauty within.

Points of Interest:
- "Forcing" is the term used for growing bulbs indoors and getting them to bloom more quickly than they would in nature.
- Bulbs have everything they need within them as far as food goes.
- The rocks and soil are used to help hold the bulbs in place. If you were to cut a bulb in half you would see the whole plant inside (not the color, however).
- These bulbs are most easily found in stores from late September through winter holidays.
- Amaryllis and paper white narcissus are tender bulbs. This means they are killed by freezing temperatures.
- If bulbs are planted toward the end of October, paper whites will bloom for Thanksgiving. Amaryllis will usually bloom sometime between Thanksgiving and New Year's Day.
- When purchasing bulbs, make sure they are firm with no mold.
- Look for amaryllis that are already showing the point of a bloom stalk to ensure bloom.

Adaptations:
- ✓ Crocus, hyacinths (see Precautions on page 97), daffodils and tulips can also be forced but they require a cool treatment of 12 weeks. This can be done in a refrigerator or by burying pots outdoors in a thick layer of mulch.
- ✓ For those impatient with waiting for flowers, add some rye grass seed to soil surface around bulbs and watch that grow. A weekly haircut will be in order.

Notes

Spring Baskets

🕐 **Time Allowed:** 60 minutes

Goal Areas:
Sensory
Fine Motor
Cognitive
Social/Emotional

Planning Notes:
✓ Start a sample of the project two weeks in advance.
✓ Do this project two weeks prior to the time bowls are to be used as table decorations.

Materials:
- Spring-colored plastic bowls
- Flower stickers
- Disposable, non-latex gloves
- Trays of pre-moistened potting mix
- Scoops
- Wheat seed
- Vermiculite
- Water in containers with sponges
- Water-proof markers
- Artificial flowers (for following week)
- Plastic eggs (for following week - optional)

Precautions:
✓ Use scoops instead of cups to transfer soil and vermiculite if working with those who might ingest the materials.

Spring Baskets

Step-by-Step Directions

1. Discuss the season, asking questions such as:
   * What season are we in?
   * What comes to mind when you think of spring?
   * What holidays are celebrated in spring?
2. Distribute plastic containers to each person and have them:
   * Write names on the bottom of the container with water-proof marker.
   * Apply stickers to the outer sides of the container.
   * Set bowl aside.
3. Distribute gloves. Mix potting mix in trays with warm water until evenly moist (not soggy).
4. Fill decorated bowl half full with moistened potting mix.
5. Sprinkle wheat seed evenly over surface.
6. Cover seed with vermiculite by pouring from the scoop.
7. Water until damp, but not floating, by squeezing water from a sponge.
8. Place planted container under light.
9. Project will sprout within the week.
10. Inform group that the baskets will be growing green wheat grass by the following week. They will be adding flowers and other decorations to it at that time.

Spring Baskets

Helpful Hints

Concepts:

- Germination.
- Seasons.

Points of Interest:

- Wheat is used in many ways. It is most commonly used in breads and noodles.
- This is a great project for discussing the season. What changes are happening in nature? What holidays happen in the spring time? These and others are good questions to ask.
- Wheat grass is full of vitamins. Many people grow wheat grass to make wheat grass juice.
- Vermiculite is actually mica, or "fools' gold," that has been mined and then heated to a very high temperature, which makes the "layered clay" expand. It is very absorbent and has been used over the years in kitty litter and insulation.

Adaptations:

- ✓ If wheat seed is not available, you can use rye grass seed. It comes up just as quickly but the blades are not as thick. Oats and barley are also good for this project.
- ✓ If no time to grow from seed, wheat grass can be purchased at health food grocery stores, rooted and ready to plant.
- ✓ Create a more natural bowl the following week by placing cut flowers into water-filled floral vials, and insert into the grassy bowl.

Notes

Bowl of Foliage

⏱ Time Allowed: 60 minutes

Planning Notes:
✓ Propagate cuttings (page 89) at least 3 weeks in advance or purchase plants.
✓ Open bags of cuttings at least 24 hours in advance of this session.

Materials:
- "Mother" plants
- Rooted cuttings (three per person)
- One 6-inch - or larger - bowl per person
- Disposable, non-latex gloves
- Potting mix in trays, moistened with hot water
- Scoops
- Gravel or stones (to cover the bottom of each bowl to a level of at least 1/2 inch)
- Aquarium charcoal (one 3-oz. cup/scoop per person)
- Water bottles filled with water
- Plastic or wood labels
- Water-proof markers
- Selection of decorative items

Precautions:
✓ Closely supervise to prevent those with cognitive difficulties from ingesting materials.
✓ Use scoops when working with those with high cognitive impairment or very young.

Bowl of Foliage

Step-by-Step Directions

1. Show the mother plants (where the cuttings came from) and explain how the project for the day is to create a dish garden using the rooted cuttings propagated from these larger plants (see Adaptations in Helpful Hints on the next page if you do not have rooted cuttings to use).
2. Discuss the term "propagation" and/or "cuttings."
3. Pass plants around for all to look at and touch.
4. Share what date the cuttings were started and invite any reminiscing about the project.
5. Divide groups into teams of two:
    a. Put on gloves.
    b. Mix warm water into a tray of potting mix until evenly moist (not too wet).
6. Distribute bowls, gravel and charcoal, instructing to:
    a. Empty the gravel into the bowl and use fingers to rake it level.
    b. Pour charcoal over the top of the gravel.
    c. Place enough moistened potting soil mix in the bowl to just cover the stones.
    d. Remove rooted cuttings from pots by tipping pots upside down and
    e. tapping on the bottom.
        Place rooted cuttings in bowl and fill the bowl loosely with soil mix. Gently tap bowl on table now and then to settle the soil.
7. Using squeeze water bottles, give each plant in the bowl two squirts of water.
8. Decorate soil surface in foliage bowl with gravel, stones or other items.
9. Write name on label with water-proof marker and place on inside edge of bowl.
10. Instructions for care:
    a. Place the Bowl of Foliage near a sunny window.
    b. Water when soil feels dry or bowl feels light weight.
    c. Trim plants to maintain desired height.

Bowl of Foliage

Helpful Hints

Concepts:

- Stem propagation.
- Watering.
- Drainage.

Points of Interest:

- See Points of Interest for the activity, *Planting Rooted Cuttings,* page 91.
- Gravel is used in dish gardens to keep the excess water away from the roots to prevent drowning the plants.
- Charcoal is used to keep the standing water "sweet," much like a charcoal filter in the kitchen "sweetens" the water by taking out impurities.

Adaptations:

- ✓ For a less messy process, place potting mix in a re-sealable plastic bag, along with some hot tap water. Squeeze out as much air as possible and re-seal. Participants mix the soil by kneading the bag, much like one would knead bread dough.
- ✓ Potted plants from a nursery/florist can be used in place of rooted cuttings. Select 4-inch pots with three plants per pot. Remove plants from pots and gently separate the roots. Place damp paper towels over the exposed roots until the plants are ready to be used. Eliminate the discussion point on propagation. Recommended plants are nerve plant, polka dot plant and peperomia.

Notes

FRESH FLOWER ACTIVITIES

Notes

Saint Paddy's Flower Faces

⏲ Time Allowed: 45 minutes

Materials:
- Sample of project
- One 6-inch clear plastic saucer per person
- Vermiculite or play sand
- Bottles or cups of warm water
- Masking tape
- Water-proof markers
- Collection of green and white flowers and greenery
- Scissors/clippers
- Craft glue
- Craft eyes
- Green chenille wires
- St. Pat's ribbon

Planning Notes
✓ Create a sample prior to session.
✓ Fill water bottles or cups with warm water just prior to start of session.
✓ Prepare ribbon decorations in advance by folding 4-inch pieces of ribbon in half and wrapping loose ends with green chenille wires.

Precautions:
✓ Count scissors/clippers before, during and after session. This is not a suitable project for those with severe cognitive challenges.

Saint Paddy's Flower Faces

Step-by-Step Directions

1. Facilitate discussion about St. Patrick's Day. Show sample of project.
2. Distribute a plastic container with a piece of masking tape on the side and a water-proof marker to each person. Have them write name on the tape.
3. Distribute a cup of vermiculite to each person:
   a. Pour the vermiculite into the plastic tray.
   b. Moisten vermiculite with a cup of warm water until damp but not floating. (If too full just hold hand over vermiculite and pour some of the water off.)
4. Provide each person two daisy mums:
   a. Stems may be pre-cut or left for participants to cut with instruction to trim stems approximately ¼-inch in length.
   b. Place the flowers in the center of the filled tray.
5. Provide each person with craft glue bottle:
   a. Apply glue to center of each mum.
   b. Place a craft eye on each glue spot.
6. Provide each person with greens:
   a. Stems may be pre-cut or left for participants to cut depending on ability levels.
   b. Place greens around edge of container with stems poked into wet vermiculite.
   c. Place St. Pat's ribbon decorations in vermiculite.
   d. Add more flowers or more greens to fill in open spaces.
7. Discuss care for the "flower face" (water every few days).
8. Lead Irish sing-a-long.

Saint Paddy's Flower Faces

Helpful Hints

Vocabulary:

- The letter "S."

Concepts:

- Vermiculite.
- Cut flower care.
- St. Patrick's Day Celebration.

Points of Interest:

- Saint Patrick died on March 17 in the year 461.
- The shamrock plant supposedly was used by St. Patrick to teach about the holy trinity because of its three leaves.
- The first St. Patrick's Day parade was held in the United States.
- The city of Chicago dyes its river green each year.
- In 2008, there were more people of Irish descent living in America than in Ireland!

Adaptations:

- ✓ Sand may be used instead of vermiculite.
- ✓ Full-sized carnations may be substituted for daisy mums.
- ✓ To add a smile to the flower face, bend a one-inch piece of red chenille wire into a U shape. Place in arrangement as seen in picture on page 111.

Notes

May Baskets

🕐 **Time Allowed:** 45 minutes

Goal Areas:
Sensory
Fine Motor
Cognitive
Language
Social/Emotional

Materials:
- Sample of project
- Selection of flowers and greens (see Helpful Hints on page 117)
- One 9-oz. plastic cup for flowers per person
- One 9-oz. plastic cup of warm water per person
- Floral "wet" foam, two blocks
- Plastic knives
- Scissors
- Pencils
- Chenille wires
- Pre-made paper cones with ribbon loops at top

Precautions:
✓ Count scissors before, during and after session.
✓ Only use non-toxic flowers.
✓ Eliminate chenille wires if they pose a safety issue.

Planning Notes:
✓ Purchase flowers, trim ends and place into water in advance.
✓ Cones are made by folding construction paper to desired shape, securing with staples and stapling on a ribbon hanger.
✓ Prepare cups of warm water just prior to session.

May Baskets

Step-by-Step Directions

1. Initiate discussion regarding the season and May Day (see Helpful Hints on next page).
2. Provide each person with:
   * Cup.
   * A piece of floral foam (one-eighth of foam block).
   * Plastic knife.
3. Trim the foam so that it fits snugly in cup.
4. Pour warm water over the top of the foam until water can be seen coming up in cup.
5. Introduce one type of flower, pass around for smelling, touching and discussion. Demonstrate how the cup and flowers will be going into a paper cone. Flower stems should be cut long in order to show.
   * Give each person some of that flower instructing to cut the stem to the desired length and place into the foam.
   (Have pre-cut when unsafe for participants to use scissors.)
6. Repeat Step 5 for each plant material.
7. Demonstrate wrapping chenille wire around pencil to make curlicue, removing pencil, stretching curlicue and placing in arrangement for decoration. Have each person follow these instructions for as many curlicues as desired.
8. Drop cup of flowers into pre-made paper cone.
9. Show off May Baskets to the group.
10. Discuss care (provide fresh water every day).
11. Discuss who might receive the May Baskets, and instruct participants to hang the floral baskets on door knobs.

May Baskets

Helpful Hints

Vocabulary:

- Names of flowers.
- Verbalize colors.

Concepts:

- May Day.
- Anonymously giving to others.
- Fresh flower care.

Points of Interest:

- White carnations will have more fragrance than colored.
- Carnations and mums will last for at least a week and often longer.
- Flowers can absorb warm water more readily than cold water.
- Cut stems on an angle for increased water absorption.
- May Day has many traditions. Ask groups of older individuals to share their memories of May Day, e.g., May Dance, May Pole, May Baskets.

Adaptations:

- ✓ Individuals can help each other by partnering, e.g., one person safely cuts while the other person holds the stems (where appropriate).
- ✓ People with minimal vision can be encouraged to use their tactile senses to note where the flowers should be placed.
- ✓ Paper cones can be made by participants depending on time and on their ability level.
- ✓ Paper for cones can be decorated prior to rolling by stamping or, after cone has been formed, using colored markers and/or stickers.

Notes

Fresh Flower Mandalas

⏰ Time Allowed: 45 minutes

Goal Areas:
Sensory
Fine Motor
Cognitive
Social/Emotional

Materials:
- Sample of project
- Pictures of mandalas and sand paintings
- Kaleidoscopes (optional)
- One 6-inch clear plastic saucer per person
- Vermiculite or play sand
- Bottles of warm water
- Masking tape
- Water-proof markers
- Collection of flowers (cut stems to 1/4-inch if not safe for participants to cut)
- Scissors/clippers

Precautions:
✓ Count scissors/clippers before, during and after session. This is not a suitable project for those with severe cognitive challenges.

Planning Notes:
✓ Create a sample prior to session.
✓ Have pictures of mandalas and sand paintings to show.
✓ Cut flowers and place in vase prior to session.
✓ Fill water bottles with warm water just prior to start of session.

Fresh Flower Mandalas

Step-by-Step Directions

1. Facilitate discussion about what a mandala is (see Helpful Hints on next page).
   * Show pictures of various mandalas and sand paintings.
   * Show sample.
   * After discussion, let everyone look through kaleidoscopes to see patterns (optional).
2. Distribute a plastic container filled with sand or vermiculite to each person.
3. Moisten vermiculite with warm water until damp but not floating. (If too full just hold hand over vermiculite and pour off some of the water.)
4. Place a variety of flowers within reach of everyone.
5. Stems may be pre-cut or left for participants to cut with instruction to trim stems almost to the bloom.
6. Instruct people to:
   a. Work in silence.
   b. Start the design in the center. Simply push the stem end of the flower into the vermiculite/sand.
   c. Continue with more flowers to create their own design.
   d. When complete, write name on masking tape and stick to side of container.
7. Instructions for care:
   * Add fresh warm water every other day.
   * Remove wilted flowers and replace with fresh at any time.

Helpful Hints

Concepts:
- Trusting oneself.
- Focusing.
- Similarities in various cultures.

Points of Interest:
- Mandala: The Sanskrit word for circle or Sacred Circle; in most traditions the mandala, a circular design, is a tool of concentration and meditation for aiding in physical, psychological and spiritual renewal.
- Some naturally occurring mandalas are cross sections of plants, the iris of the eye, centers of flowers, and snowflakes.
- Vermiculite is actually mica, or "fools' gold," a layered clay that has been mined and then heated to a very high temperature, which makes the "layered clay" expand. It is very absorbent and has been used over the years as kitty litter and insulation.
- Warm water is more easily taken up by cut flowers than cold water.

Adaptations:
✓ If the concept of the mandala is not appropriate for your setting, simply change to the idea of the kaleidoscope. Individuals will be creating a picture using flowers to represent what they might see when looking through a kaleidoscope.
✓ The project can also be adapted for a seasonal experience: red, white and green for Christmas, red and white for Valentine's, etc.

Notes

Seasonal Bouquets

⏱ Time Allowed: 45 minutes

Planning Notes:
✓ Prep flowers in advance by trimming stems and placing in warm water with preservative.

Materials:
- Selection of flowers and greens (see Helpful Hints on page 125)
- One decorative cup per person
- Floral "wet" foam, two blocks
- Plastic knives
- Scissors/pruners
- Warm water in separate cups
- Seasonal decorations
- Masking tape
- Water-proof markers

Precautions:
✓ For people with severe cognitive and/or emotional deficits, or the very young, avoid using floral foam. Instead, make a criss-cross grid of masking tape on cup to hold flowers.
✓ Count scissors before, during and after session.
✓ Only use non-toxic flowers.

Seasonal Bouquets

Step-by-Step Directions

1. Open with discussion of the current season and the holiday that is near. Initiate reminiscing of that holiday/season. Share regarding making flower arrangements.
2. Provide each person with a cup.
   a. Stick a piece of masking tape to each cup.
   b. Write names (as able) on tape, using markers.
   c. Trim a block of floral foam to fit snugly in cup.
3. Add warm water to top of foam until water can be seen coming up inside cup.
4. Introduce one type of flower, pass around for smelling, touching and discussion.
5. Give each person some of that flower instructing to cut stems to the desired length (no taller than two cup heights).
   a. Repeat for each plant material.
   b. Add any seasonal decorations.
7. Provide the opportunity for showing off the arrangements.
8. Discuss care (add fresh warm water daily).
9. Discuss whether flowers will be kept or given away. If given away, who might be the recipients?

Seasonal Bouquets

Helpful Hints

Vocabulary:
- Names of flowers.
- Verbalize colors.

Concepts:
- Height relationships.
- Fresh flower care.

Points of Interest:
- White carnations are often more fragrant than colored.
- Carnations and mums will last for one or more weeks.
- Flowers can absorb warm water more readily than cold water due to reduced surface tension.
- Flowers absorb more water when stems are cut on an angle.
- Any of the following items will help your cut flowers last longer:
  - ✳ Floral preservative from florist.
  - ✳ Small amount of lemon lime soda in water (not diet soda!).

Adaptations:
- ✓ Individuals can help each other by partnering, e.g., one person safely cuts while the other person holds the stems.
- ✓ People with minimal vision can be encouraged to use their tactile senses to note where the flowers should be placed.

Notes

Say It With Flowers

! **Time Allowed:** 45 minutes

Materials:

- Sample of project
- Selection of flowers and herbs (see Helpful Hints on page 129)
- Two 6-inch paper doilies with 1-inch "X" cut in center per person
- Thin ribbon cut to one-foot length per person
- Damp paper towels
- One 6x6-inch square of aluminum foil per person
- Prepared gift cards that tell the name and meaning of each plant and have a hole punched in one corner
- Scissors

Precautions:

✓ Count scissors before, during and after session.
✓ Always use non-toxic plants.

Planning Notes:

✓ Purchase herbs and flowers if fresh grown not available.
✓ Create a sample of project just prior to session.
✓ Create cards in advance that list the names of the plant materials and their meaning.

Say It With Flowers

Step-by-Step Directions

1. Show an example of the project, a "Tussie Mussie," and share the information about its history from the Helpful Hints on the next page.
2. Provide each person with two prepared doilies, one on top of the other.
3. Show a carnation and share with group the meaning of the flower. Hand out one carnation to each person, inviting them to:
    a. Place the stem through the hole in the doilies.
    b. Smell the bloom.
4. Follow Step 3 for each plant material you will be using.
5. When arrangement is done:
    a. Fold damp paper toweling around stem ends to prevent drying out.
    b. Wrap aluminum foil around the damp paper toweling and the center of the doilies. This creates a ruffled look around the flowers.
    c. Thread ribbon through the hole in the card.
    d. Tie ribbon and card around top of foil, just under doily.
6. Encourage discussion about sharing the "Tussie Mussie" with someone; who and why?

Say It With Flowers

Helpful Hints

Concepts:

- Life before sanitation/diseases, personal hygiene.
- Times prior to greeting cards.

Points of Interest:

- "Tussie Mussies" originated in medieval times when herbs with medicinal fragrances were used to cover the dirt floors and thought to combat germs and fight diseases such as the plague.
- Ladies and men during those times would hold a handful of herbs to their noses when going out into garbage-filled streets.
- This little bouquet became known as a "nosegay," or in the medieval language, a "Tussie Mussie."
- The language of flowers came to England in the 1700s, but its origin goes back to the Middle East where the Turks sent fruit and floral greetings, which represented a verse of classical poetry. This was called "floriography." Once in Europe, the concept was altered by giving each plant a different symbolism. These meanings would vary according to use, growing characteristics or religious significance, so one plant would often have several messages.
- During the Victorian era, "Tussie Mussies" were at their peak and the type of communication was called the "language of flowers." No fine lady was ever seen without her "Tussie Mussie."
- Fancy hankies, or even "posy holders" made of gold, silver, silver plate, or brass, were used in Victorian times.
- There are a number of books on this topic available in libraries.
- Suitable plant materials are:
  * Carnations: love returned
  * Daisies: beauty, innocence
  * Marigolds: joy, remembrance, friendship
  * Lavender: devotion

Helpful Hints Continued

* Strawflowers: never ceasing remembrance
* Rose: love
* Scented geraniums (citrus): unexpected meeting
* Parsley: festivity, joy
* Thyme: happiness
* Rosemary: remembrance

Adaptations:

✓ For someone with the use of only one hand:
  * Tape a cup securely to the table. Place double-stick tape along top edge of cup in several places and then lay prepared doilies on top of cup. This should hold all in place while individual places materials through hole in doilies. When arrangement is completed, gently lift off of cup and wrap as directed.
✓ If people are going to keep the bouquet for themselves, they might want to eliminate wrapping the stems and just set atop a glass of water.
✓ For high-functioning groups:
  * Have them select from a variety of plant materials and also make the cards.
  * Group can also make up the meanings for the flowers.

Carnation Corsages

⏱ **Time Allowed:** 60 minutes

Goal Areas:
Sensory
Fine Motor
Gross Motor
Cognitive
Social/Emotional

Materials:
- Sample of project
- Two white mini carnations with stems cut to one inch per person
- 20-gauge, or higher, floral wire
- Green floral tape
- Chenille wires (two per person)
- Ribbon (3 feet per person)
- Scissors/clippers
- Pencils
- Safety pins or corsage pins
- Styrofoam cups or heavy tape (if using corsage pins)

Precautions:
✓ Count scissors before, during and after session.
✓ Cover end of corsage pin at completion to avoid potential injury.
✓ This project is not for use with those who have high levels of confusion.

Planning Notes:
✓ Prep flowers in advance by trimming ends and placing in warm water with floral preservative.
✓ Pre-cut:
  - Floral wire (two 6-inch pieces each)
  - Ribbon
  - Floral tape (one-foot each)
✓ Create sample corsage, keep fresh in refrigerator.

Carnation Corsages

Step-by-Step Directions

1. Initiate discussion around corsages; memories of corsages for dances, weddings, other special occasions; what flowers were they made from?
2. Show a sample of the finished corsage.
3. Provide each participant two carnations, wires and tape.
4. Run a 6-inch piece of wire through the green base (calyx) of one carnation.
5. Repeat Step 4 with second carnation.
6. Holding the two carnations together, with one slightly higher than the other, wrap wires with about 3 inches of floral tape. Staff will need to start the tape for participants to ensure it is held tightly at top.
7. Make bow (see Helpful Hints on next page for instructions).
8. Place bow directly under the bottom flower and wrap wire around stem.
9. Hand out chenille wires, pencils, and floral tape:
   a. Curl chenille around pencil leaving 1 inch, uncurled, at end.
   b. Pull the chenille off pencil and pull slightly to extend curls.
   c. Repeat with other chenille.
10. Place curled chenille pieces at the back of the corsage and hold in place.
11. Wrap stems and chenille with floral tape. Staff or volunteers may need to start this step.
12. Curl wrapped stem around pencil to corkscrew, pull gently to loosen, remove pencil.
13. Pin on with either safety pins or corsage pins. If using corsage pins, put small piece of styrofoam cup or heavy tape on point of pin as a pin guard.

Carnation Corsages

Helpful Hints

Concepts:
- Corsages.

Points of Interest:
- Mini carnations are a hybrid of the larger, standard carnation.
- Traditionally, men wear *boutonnieres*.
- Corsages will stay fresh, when not worn, if placed in a plastic bag and lightly sprayed with water.

Adaptations:
- ✓ For individuals with the use of only one hand, partner them with another person. Have one hold the flower, etc., while the other places the wire or wraps the stems.
- ✓ The project could be made and wrapped with floral tape to a hair clip for a hair adornment, or wrapped to a band of elastic for a wrist corsage.
- ✓ Omit the bow if someone chooses to make a *boutonniere*.

Bow Instructions:
- Person A holds both pointer fingers up with about 3 inches between them.
- Person B wraps length of ribbon around the other's fingers.
- Staff wraps floral wire tightly around the middle of ribbon.

Notes

FOOD ACTIVITIES

Notes

Herbal Hour

⏲ Time Allowed: 60 minutes

Goal Areas:
Sensory
Fine Motor
Cognitive
Language
Social/Emotional

Materials:
- One small package of whipped cream cheese
- Small container plain yogurt
- Crackers/bread
- Cucumbers
- Variety of herbs (chives, parsley, dill)
- One small bowl for each spread made
- Two bowls with cool water
- Paper towels
- Spoons
- Plastic knives
- Cutting boards
- Clean kitchen scissors
- Dried or fresh mint
- Glass iced tea container
- Four tea bags
- Cups, plates, napkins
- Hand sanitizer
- Food-handler gloves
- Serving plates

Precautions:
✓ Check on dietary restrictions.
✓ Count scissors before, during and after session.

Planning Notes:
✓ If using herbs and cucumbers from the garden, cut the morning of the session.
✓ Purchase herbs/veggies (if not grown), other food items and tableware within one or two days prior to session.
✓ Make sun tea and cool a day before session.

Herbal Hour

Step-by-Step Directions

1. Begin with discussion about herbs (see Helpful Hints on next page).
2. Pass pieces of each herb around for a sensory experience.
3. Divide group into two teams:

    * Cream Cheese Team:
        a. All apply hand sanitizer and put on food handler gloves.
        b. Wash herbs in bowl of water and pat dry with paper towels.
        c. Using spoon, divide cream cheese between two small bowls.
        d. Cut up chives and place in one bowl.
        e. Cut up parsley and place in other bowl.
        f. Stir herbs into cream cheese.
        g. Spread on crackers or bread.
        h. Place on serving plate.

    * Yogurt Team:
        a. All apply hand sanitizer and put on food handler gloves.
        b. Wash herbs in bowl of water and pat dry with paper towels.
        c. Place yogurt in bowl.
        d. Chop dill and place in bowl with yogurt.
        e. Cut cucumber slices and set on plate.

4. Serve all, along with the sun tea, and perhaps play some soft music.

Herbal Hour

Helpful Hints

Points of Interest:

- Parsley: In ancient Greece it was believed that one could drink without getting drunk if wearing a wreath of parsley. It contains lots of Vitamin C. In the early days in Salem, MA, parsley growing in a garden was a sign of the owner being a witch.
- Chives: From China. Used as far back as 1,000 years ago and described in the writings of Marco Polo. Called the "Jewel of the Orient."
- Dill: Called the "Meet'n Seed" from the practice of women giving it to their babies and young children to chew during long church services to keep them quiet. Dill is from the Norse word for "to dull."

Adaptations:

✓ The session could be expanded by creating any of the following:
  * Herbal oils.
  * Herbal ice cubes.
  * Herbal teas.
  Recipes arc available on the internet and books on herbs.

Notes

Hawaiian Hour I

⏱ **Time Allowed:** 60 minutes

Goal Areas:
Sensory
Fine Motor
Gross Motor
Cognitive
Social/Emotional

Materials:
- Two of each: papaya, mango pineapple, banana, coconut
- Small plates and napkins
- Small cups
- Blender and extension cord
- Ice
- Piña colada mix
- Gloves for servers
- Knife/cutting board
- Plastic bags
- Hawaiian music
- CD player
- Leis
- Food-handler gloves

Precautions:
✓ Check with dietary or nursing re: any food restrictions for participants and adapt as necessary.
✓ Some people have an allergic reaction to touching the fruit of the mango. Only have people wearing gloves handle the fruit extensively.

Planning Notes:
✓ Purchase papayas, mangoes and pineapple several days in advance to ensure ripeness for session.
✓ Cut up one of each of the fruit and place in individual containers prior to start of session.

Hawaiian Hour I

Step-by-Step Directions

1. Have soft Hawaiian music playing in the background and place a lei around each person's neck as they arrive at the session, greeting them with "Aloha."

   a. Start out with, "Today we are going on a short trip to Hawaii. You will be trying lots of interesting foods you can find there. In another session we will plant what we saved from the food we have eaten, growing what we can call our Hawaiian kitchen garden."

   b. Invite people to share their memories or thoughts of Hawaii.

2. Pass around papaya, letting everyone touch and smell, and discuss it using information from Helpful Hints on the next page.

   a. Pass pre-cut papaya for all to sample.

   b. Repeat Step 2 with the rest of the fruits.
   (Save all the seeds and pineapple top. Place in plastic bags after class. Refrigerate for at least 2 weeks but no more than one month)

3. In a blender, puree fruit, drink mix and ice. Serve and enjoy while listening to music.

4. As music plays, teach several easy hula hand motions and/or encourage the group to create movements for palm trees, waves, birds, sunshine, rain, etc.

5. At completion of session, collect leis explaining they will be used at the next Hawaiian Hour (optional).

Hawaiian Hour I

Helpful Hints

Points of Interest

- Coconut: Grows in palm trees. The part we see and buy in the store is the inside of a larger shell that is big and green. Inside the coconut is a fluid often called "coconut milk," though it is not the same as canned coconut milk.
- Papaya: Also known as pawpaw. It is delicious as a fruit but is also used for papain which is the dried, purified latex of the papaya. Papain is used in meat tenderizers, chewing gum, clarifying fruit juices, stabilizing beer, toothpaste brighteners, and skin lotions/freckle removers. Some people are allergic to papaya so always check first before serving.
- Mango: Native to N.E. India, Burma and Thailand; 4,000 years under cultivation. The juice of the skin can often cause a rash.
- Pineapple: Native to Brazil and Paraguay. Some say Columbus first named in 1493 because he thought it looked like a large pine cone ... name derived from the Spanish word *piña*. Pineapple tops are most successfully grown if the top is twisted off instead of cut off. Have one person hold the bottom while another twists off the top.
- Banana: Bananas are often grown in a process called "division" where the new plant comes from the "mother" plant's roots. The seeds in the bananas we most commonly eat are sterile. Bananas grow in bunches on the plants and the bunches grow with the fruit pointing up.

Adaptations:

✓ To prepare the coconut for eating, use a screwdriver, hammer and tray. Pound screwdriver into the "eye" of the coconut.

Notes

Hawaiian Hour II

(!) ⏱ **Time Allowed:** 60 minutes

Goal Areas:
Fine Motor
Gross Motor
Sensory
Cognitive
Language
Social/Emotional

Planning Notes:
✓ Do this within one month after the Hawaiian Hour I session, page 141.
✓ Use seeds from Hawaiian Hour I.

Materials:
- Seeds and top from Hawaiian Hour I.
- Four 8-oz. foam cups
- Three bins of potting mix
- Three water bottles with warm water
- Two 6-inch pots
- Bins for watering
- Water-proof markers
- Tape or labels
- Pencils
- Re-sealable gallon-size plastic bags
- Toothbrush and bowl of water
- Disposable, non-latex gloves

Precautions:
✓ Some people have an allergic reaction to touching the fruit of the mango. Only have people wearing gloves handle the seed extensively.

Hawaiian Hour II

Step-by-Step Directions

1. At the beginning of the session explain this is Part Two of a two-part project.
2. This project is planting the seeds from what was taste tested in the Hawaiian Hour I session. Begin by showing the seeds/tops, etc., from that session.
3. Divide the group into three teams:

* Papaya Team:
   a. Provide each person in team with a foam cup and water-proof marker.
   b. Write his/her name, "Papaya," and the date on the outside of cup.
   c. Poke drainage holes in the cup bottom using a pencil.
   d. Provide the team with a tray of moistened potting mix and have them work in the water until there is no more dry soil.
   e. Fill the cups with potting mix to within ¼-inch of the top.
   f. Using pencils, make one hole in mix for each seed (3-4 seeds per cup).
   g. Squeeze aril (protective coating) off of seed.
   h. Drop seeds in holes and cover with mix.
   i. Set in pan and water/drain.
   j. Place in re-sealable plastic bag.
      1. Seal bag leaving a small opening at one end.
      2. Place drinking straw in bag opening.
      3. Blow through the straw, filling the bag with air until it expands fully like a balloon.
      4. Quickly remove the straw and seal the bag.
      5. Place under lights or in a warm window sill.
   k. When green sprouts begin to show, open the bags and let them sit open for 24 hours before removing the plants from the bags (germination time is 1 to 3 months).

Step-by-Step Directions Continued

* Mango Team:
  a. Have one team member wear gloves and scrub mango pit with a toothbrush in a bowl of water to remove any excess flesh for easier handling.
  b. Using the tip of a spoon, gently pry the furry coat of the pit open and remove the bean-shaped seed inside.
  c. Provide the team with a tray of moistened potting mix and have them work in the water until there is no more dry soil.
  d. Fill a 4-inch pot three-quarters full of potting mix.
  e. Place the mango seed on a slight angle in the pot and cover with soil mix, leaving the tip of the seed exposed.
  f. Water potted seed, allowing excess to drain out.
  g. Place potted/drained seed into gallon-size re-sealable plastic bag.
  h. Follow Steps 1-5 from Papaya Team on previous page.
  i. Open bag as soon as a sprout emerges. Leave potted mango seed in the open bag for at least 24 hours to acclimate to the dry environment.

* Pineapple Team:
  a. Have one person remove the leaves off the bottom 1½ inches of the pineapple top.
  b. Provide the team with a tray of moistened potting mix and have them work in the water until there is no more dry soil.
  c. Fill a 6-inch pot full of potting mix.
  d. Stick the bare end of top into the soil-filled pot, firming the soil around the top.
  e. Label with the date, names of the team and name of plant.
  f. Water and place under lights or in a sunny window.

Hawaiian Hour II

Helpful Hints

Language:
- "S" sounds.

Concepts:
- New plants from old.

Points of Interest:
- Papaya seeds are surrounded by a sac called an aril. This protective coating must be removed before the seed can germinate. Just squeeze and rub the seed with fingers to remove the aril.
- Mangoes are very slow to germinate and sometimes never do. Therefore, it is best to plant this as an experiment.
- Pineapple tops are most successfully grown if the top is twisted off instead of cut off. On day one, have one person hold the bottom while another twists the top off. If the top is already cut, remove as much of the fruit as possible to avoid rotting.

Adaptations:
- ✓ Incorporate Hawaiian music in the background.
- ✓ Samples of each fruit could help participants relate the connections between the seeds and the fruit.

APPENDIXES

APPENDIX A
MODELS FOR HORTICULTURAL-BASED ACTIVITIES

Choosing Activities
There are many factors to consider when choosing activities. Some of these include the participants, the setting and the staff.

Factors Related to the Participants
- What are the ability/developmental levels?
- Recognize the differences/ability levels across the domains.
- Are you working toward achievement of an objective or mastering a goal?
- What are the interests/motivations of the participants?

Factors Related to the Setting
- Is it a clinical, care community, school, or home setting, etc?
- Is the physical environment appropriate for the activity?
- Are resources, such as a water source, a light source and storage, available to support the activities?
- What is the time allotted for the project?
- What takes place before and after the session in the activity space and in the facility?
- Can the activity address the participants' goals/curriculum?

Factors Related to Staff
- Will there be sufficient staff/volunteers for the activity?
- Are staff/volunteers appropriately trained?
- Are staff/volunteers enthusiastic about using horticultural-based activities?

Transitioning Between Activities
In settings which serve individuals with short/poor attending skills, careful planning and attention to the steps involved in the task can make transitions much easier. Some ideas which may help provide smooth transitions include:
- Timing of transitions is extremely important. Move participants to the next activity before they lose interest. When more than half of the group give the "I'm finished" signal, it's time to move on to the next activity. Moving on too quickly, however, can be very frustrating and upsetting for some participants. Invite those who are clearly ready to move on to be helpers or to transition first. This will give extra attention and/or time to those who need it.
- Sequencing of activities into separate sessions provides opportunities for more in-depth projects. Building transitions into your activities is a natural and effective way to move from one session to another. For example: Session one would involve gathering leaves and flowers. Session two would be the *Preserving Flowers and Leaves* activity, page 32. Session three would be decorating cards or the *Fall Leaf Window Art* activity, page 43.
- Demonstrating and discussing the next activity after the participants have finished the previous one will help participants with memory deficits to mentally separate from the earlier activity. This provides a space between the projects, which tends to create a smoother transition.
- Provide visual closure to activities by gathering/cleaning up materials and simultaneously have another adult introduce the next activity. This is particularly important when working with individuals with high levels of cognitive impairment.

APPENDIX B
CREATING THE TEAM

Recruiting

Team building is an important aspect of any successful program. Therapists, paraprofessionals, staff, family members, and volunteers come together for a common purpose: to plan and provide therapeutic services. These activities provide opportunities for participants to work toward achieving their goals and objectives in a unique therapeutic setting. In this approach, it's through horticultural-based activities. The teams may vary in size, with only one facilitator and an aide or volunteer, or a team could consist of a very comprehensive group of professionals, such as a special education teacher, physical therapist, occupational therapist, social worker, counselor, nurse, speech and language pathologist, activities professional, and/or horticultural therapist.

Clinical settings, in particular, use multi-disciplinary teams. Each member of such a group would share from his/her area of expertise. The team collaboratively works toward the shared purpose of planning and providing effective intervention services for those they serve.

When "the team" consists of a therapist, related staff and/or volunteers, again, they work in a collaborative manner; however, the therapist takes the lead, providing guidance, stability and knowledge.

Characteristics to Look for When Selecting Team Members
- A clear understanding of the role of the horticultural component: The primary focus is the participant and the individual's needs/goals. Plants are simply a means to an end.
- Flexibility: Unpredictable events occur in nature; they also occur with participants, staff, weather, and outside events/activities.
- Commitment: This includes reliability and a sincere interest to grow along with the participants.
- Independent work ethic: This is characterized by the understanding of the organization's policies and the ability to work with minimal supervision in both an independent and cooperative manner.

Team Training, Building and Maintenance

Each member brings his/her own skills, abilities and strengths to the team. Volunteers have areas of expertise and strengths to contribute. A combination and blending of these skills can create an ideal basis for training. A variety of training formats can be utilized including:
- Basic information, strategies and terminology from each discipline, should be provided and reviewed. Training sessions should be collaborative and cooperative in content and spirit.
- Orientations for new team members.
- "Brain Storming" meetings to review current practices and possible changes.
- "Review and Redo" time at the conclusion of each session.

"Renew" periodically to ensure that all team members share the same goals, knowledge, interest in growth, and feel like an important member of the team.

Matching volunteers' strengths with program needs is one step in maintaining a volunteer team. Demonstrating appreciation is another vital aspect. Find ways to let volunteers/staff know they are valuable and make a difference.

APPENDIX C
ADAPTING HORTICULTURAL-BASED ACTIVITIES TO MEET SPECIFIC NEEDS

Activities can be modified as an effective means of accommodating a group of participants with various ability levels to interact together in the same environment. This can be accomplished by adapting the environment, substituting materials, using only parts of activities, using parallel techniques, and adjusting the type or amount of facilitation provided.

Adapting the Environment
- Accessibility to the work environment, such as the height of tables or gardens, is extremely important when serving people with reduced mobility, including those in wheelchairs. Being able to easily reach the work surface is not only fundamental to participation, it is also fundamental to a participant's sense of inclusion and success.
- No sink in the room: Fill a large drink dispenser with warm water.
- No storage: Create a rolling supply cart that will hold the items needed for session.
- Proper lighting: This is critical for plant propagation. Artificial lighting can be provided either through purchasing or building tiered light carts that use fluorescent lights. More information on these light carts can be found at www.ahta.org or through companies listed in the Resources Appendix (Appendix H, page 158). Instructions for making your own lighting setup can be obtained through many on-line sources.

Substituting Materials
Substituting or adding materials can be one of the easiest ways to accommodate different age groups or ability levels within a group. Simple changes, such as the following, are steps in enhancing a project's success:
- Creating a grid of floral or masking tape over the opening of a cup instead of using floral foam in the container protects those who might ingest the materials during a floral arranging session.
- Adding fun stickers to pots is a means of more fully engaging children in a planting activity.
- In a short-stay program, dividing pots of rooted plants for use in dish gardens, etc., vs. needing to start cuttings three weeks earlier for the project.

Using Adaptive Equipment
There are many types of adaptive tools available from mail order companies. Assessing what type of adaptation an individual requires will determine what tool(s) should be purchased or modified. Often the individuals being served will be the best guides as to what works for them. Some simple and inexpensive adaptive tools are:
- Loop scissors
- Extended water wands
- Lightweight tools
- Universal cuffs
- Small scoops

Using Elements of an Activity
No matter how well we plan or try to provide activities which are appropriate, there will be times when one or more of the participants cannot fully engage in the activity with any success. These times, though infrequent, need to be planned for and addressed with ease. Recognize which elements of an activity an individual can engage in with some success. From this assessment make the appropriate changes, such as paralleling or adjusting facilitation. There will be times when a participant may need to be seen on an individual basis with only limited parts of the activity presented at one session.

Parallel Techniques

There will be times when a participant is not capable of doing the same exact activity as the rest of the group. You may know this beforehand and plan accordingly or you may need to modify in the middle of the activity. For example, if an individual cannot tolerate touching the materials used in potting mix, an easy solution would be to provide gloves or a trowel, therefore, reducing their tactile or sensory defensiveness.

Adjusting Facilitation

Modifying the amount or type of facilitation is another means of adapting activities. Some participants may be able to complete an activity independently, while others may need minimal assistance, such as verbal cues. Still others may need complete support, such as step-by-step verbal instruction and even hand-over-hand assistance.

Substituting Materials

Substituting materials can be one of the easiest ways to accommodate different age groups or ability levels within a group. Simple changes, such as using loop "snips" instead of scissors, can make all the difference to a participant with a physical challenge or limited fine motor coordination.

APPENDIX D
HORTICULTURAL-BASED ACTIVITIES AND MEMORY CARE

Horticultural-based projects are ideal for individuals with Alzheimer's or other forms of memory loss. For many people, gardening and working with plants was a part of early life, often done with family members, especially parents and grandparents. Due to this connection to long term memory, the required skills for working with plants, arranging flowers, and gardening, can remain long into the life of the participants/residents.

Another benefit of many horticultural-based activities is that they can be broken down into more basic tasks that even those with advanced cognitive deficits are able to accomplish somewhat independently. Examples of this are mixing soil, filling pots with soil or watering with assistance.

The goals of this population tend to be focused on maintaining abilities and life enrichment rather than on development and improvement of skills. The plant activities can provide opportunities for participants to show off their creativity, making something suitable and age-appropriate for gifting to others. Through the physical aspect of the projects, the continued use and exercise of fine and gross motor skills supports a healthy body. Through carefully selected and structured projects, a greater sense of self esteem is obtained.

Sensory stimulation is effective in assisting individuals to remain connected to their outer world. Most horticultural activities create a means for that experience. Plants with interesting textures, fragrances (for those who still have olfactory senses), tastes, bright colors, and patterns, are all excellent additions to the horticultural component. Projects such as *Herbal Hour*, page 137, and *Holiday Sachets*, page 47, are examples of specific sessions that have a sensory focus. Every activity, however, can have within it a sensory element.

There are certain precautions that must be adhered to when serving this population, such as:
- Use only non-toxic plants (see Appendix I, page 160), fertilizers, pest control and craft supplies. If unsure, look it up. There are many resources for determining the safety of plants and plant care, and craft items will specify on the label whether they are safe.
- Keep an eye on sharp objects, such as scissors, and anything permanent, such as markers. Take a count at the beginning, during and, again, at the end of a session.
- Provide one-on-one attention to anyone who might ingest materials. To assist with preventing the confusion, resulting in ingesting soil and plants, avoid using supplies that resemble eating utensils. Use pots instead of cups to plant in, scoops instead of spoons for moving soil, and water cans instead of cups or bottles for water for watering. If possible, avoid doing planting projects at the dining table. It is only natural in this setting that those with high levels of confusion would mistakenly think the soil and plants were for eating.

APPENDIX E
MONITORING THE HORTICULTURAL-BASED ACTIVITY PROGRAM

Developing a System of Evaluation

A form of monitoring is required to ensure the horticultural component is meeting people's needs. Consistent charting will provide a means of tracking the status of participants' outcomes and can "red flag" any significant changes and/or concerns. Examining and assessing each activity will help to determine which strategies are working and which ones need adjustments. Along with program enhancement, charting can provide valuable documentation and/or data. This is important when writing care conference reports, applying for grants, or when needing to provide program justification and support for the budget. Following is an example of a simple chart that could be used for documentation after a session.

THERAPIST: _____ INTERNS/VOLUNTEERS: _____

SITE: _____ DATE: _____ TIME: _____

ACTIVITY: _____

OUTCOMES:
1) Remained attentive to discussion during session for at least 15 minutes.
2) Utilized FM and/or GM skills for a minimum of 10 minutes.
3) Experienced sensory stimulation with at least 3 items.

KEY: **O.** (outcome status), **PART.** (participation), **ASSIST.** (assistance)
OUTCOME STATUS: + (met), = (partially met), **0** (not met)
SCALE: 0-5 with 5 = highest level

NAME	O. 1	O. 2	O. 3	PART.	ASSIST.	COMMENTS

COMMENTS: _____
_____
_____
_____

_____   _____
Charter's signature and credentials   Date

APPENDIX F
EXAMPLES OF GOALS AND OBJECTIVES

Goal: Experience increased sensory stimulation.
Objective: Participant will engage in sensory stimulation for a minimum of 10 minutes per session at least 2 x month.
HT short-term goal: Participant will engage in interaction with facilitator regarding: items on the sensory cart for at least 10 minutes per session at least 2 x month.

Goal: Increase/maintain fine motor skills.
Objective: Participant will engage in use of fine motor skills for at least 15 minutes at least 1 x week.
HT short-term goal: Participant will pot up plants with assistance from the facilitator, for at least 15 minutes during the HT session.

Goal: Increase/maintain gross motor skills.
Objective: Participant will utilize upper gross motor skills for a period of at least 10 minutes during the garden program at least 1 x week.
HT short-term goal: Participant will engage upper gross motor skills while mixing soil with warm water for at least 10 minutes during a garden session.

Goal: Increase/maintain level of socialization.
Objective: Participant will take part in garden group activity for 1 hour at least 3 x month.
HT short-term goal: Participant will partner with another while mixing soil and planting for at least 10 minutes during one hour group session.

Goal: Increase/maintain emotional state of well being.
Objective: Participant will create something suitable for giving.
HT short-term goal: Participant will create a holiday floral arrangement during the garden session to give as a gift.

Goal: Increase/maintain cognitive skill level.
Objective: Participant will demonstrate use of cognitive skills during garden session at least 1 x week.
HT short-term goal: Participant will name at least three common flowers from the garden during the discussion time in the garden program.

Goal: To improve language pronunciation skills.
Objective: Participant will practice word pronunciation during garden session at least 2 x month.
HT short-term goal: Participant will verbalize nature/plant related words with the "S" sound at least 3 x during the garden session.

More and more communities are practicing what is called, "Person-Directed Care." In these settings, goals would be written in the "I" format. A goal such as "Participant will utilize GM skills for a minimum of 10 minutes at least 3 x week," might instead read, "I like to garden and gardening several days a week for short amounts of time would be ideal."

APPENDIX G
PROGRAM PLANNING RESOURCES

American Horticultural Therapy Association (AHTA)
800-634-1603
www.ahta.org

National Gardening Association
800-538-7476
Fax: 802-864-6889
www.garden.org
www.kidsgardening.com

GRANTS PROGRAMS
Youth Garden Grants (see National Gardening Assoc.)

BOOKS/JOURNALS
AHTA: Journal of Therapeutic Horticulture and topic "fact" sheets available by order at www.ahta.org

Gardening Projects for Horticultural Therapy Programs (2000); Hank Bruce; Petals and Pages; (125pp)

Generations Gardening Together (2006); Jean M. Larson and Mary Hockenberry Meyer; Food Products Press; (91pp)

Health Through Horticulture: A Guide for Using the Outdoor Garden for Therapeutic Outcomes, (2003); Maria Gabaldo, M.Ed., HTR, OTR, Maryellen D. King, M.A., HTR, Eugene A. Rothert, HTR; Chicago Horticultural Society; (56pp)

Horticultural Therapy Methods; Making Connections in Health Care, Human Service, and Community Programs (2006); Rebecca Haller, HTM and Christine Kramer editors; CRC Press; (163pp)

Horticulture as Therapy: A Practical Guide to Using Horticulture as a Therapeutic Tool (1994); Mitchell Hewson, HTM; Homewood Health Centre, Inc.; 150 Delhi Street, Guelph, Ontario N1E 6K9 Canada (153pp)

Horticulture as Therapy: Principles and Practice. (1997); Sharon P. Simson, Ph.D. and Martha C. Strauss, HTR, Editors; Haworth Press; (478pp)

Indoor Nature & Plant Craft Activities (2006); Maureen A. Phillips, HTM & Sheila B. Taft, HTR; www.phillipstaft.com; (188pp)

APPENDIX H
HORTICULTURAL AND NATURE ART RESOURCES

<u>Local:</u>
Nurseries/greenhouses, garden clubs, college greenhouses

American Horticultural Society
800-777-7931
www.ahs.org

National Gardening Association
800-538-7476
Fax: 802-864-6889
www.garden.org

Cooperative Extension Service/Master Gardener Programs
www.csrees.usda.gov/Extension

TOOLS, EQUIPMENT, SEEDS, SUPPLIES

AM Leonard Inc.
800-543-8955
www.AMleo.com
tools, storage bins

America the Beautiful Fund
www.freeseed.org (to download request form)
www.america-the-beautiful.org/
free seed, information

Charley's Greenhouse
800-322-4707
www.charleysgreenhouse.com
greenhouse & propagation supplies

Improvements Catalog
800 634-9484
www.ImprovementsCatalog.com
tools, garden items

Patterson Medical
800-323-5547
www.pattersonmedical.com
adaptive tools

Gardener's Supply Company
800-427-3363
www.gardeners.com
tools, light stands, garden supplies

Gardens Alive!
513-354-1482
www.gardensalive.com
organic pest control/garden products

Hummert International
800-325-3055
www.hummert.com
wholesale commercial grower/greenhouse supplies

Lee Valley Tools, LTD
800-871-8158
www.leevalley.com
many tools adapted for raised bed gardening, potting trays, light stands

Park Seed Wholesale
800-213-0076
info@parkseed.com
www.parkseed.com
seeds, plugs/grower supplies

Plow and Hearth Products for Country Living
800-627-1712
www.plow-hearth.com

Seeds of Change
888-762-7333
www.seedsofchange.com
organic, heirloom, specialty seeds

White Flower Farm
www.whiteflowerfarm.com
seeds, plants, garden supplies

NATURE ART

Columbia Pine Cones and Botanicals
888-470-6989
www.pinecones.com
pinecones, boughs, mosses, etc.

San Francisco Herb Co.
800-227-4530
www.sfherb.com
wholesale, potpourri ingredients, recipes, herbs and spices (minimum order required)

S&S
800-288 9941
www.ssww.com
crafts, games, activities for therapy and rehabilitation, healthcare products, misc.

Oriental Trading Company
800-875-8480
www.orientaltrading.com
specialty supplies

APPENDIX I
Non-Poisonous and Poisonous Plants
(INFORMATION FROM NATIONAL CAPITAL POISON CENTER)

If you have a plant and it is not listed below, check with a poison control center to confirm it is safe prior to use.

Non-Poisonous Plants

Common Name	Botanical Name
African violet	*Saintpaulia ionantha*
Begonia	*Begonia*
Christmas cactus	*Schlumbergera bridgesii*
Coleus	*Coleus*
Dandelion	*Taraxacum officinale*
Dracaena	*Dracaena*
Forsythia	*Forsythia*
Impatiens	*Impatiens*
Jade	*Crassula argentea*
Marigold	*Tagetes*
Petunia	*Petunia*
Poinsettia	*Euphorbia pulcherrima* (may cause irritation only)
Rose	*Rosa*
Spider plant	*Chlorophytum comosum*
Swedish ivy	*Plectranthus australis*
Spiderwort	*Tradescantia*
Wild strawberry	*Fragaria virginiensis*

Poisonous Plants

Common Name	Botanical Name
Azalea, rhododendron	*Rhododendron*
Caladium	*Caladium*
Castor bean	*Ricinis communis*
Daffodil	*Narcissus*
Deadly nightshade	*Atropa belladonna*
Dumbcane	*Dieffenbachia*
Elephant ear	*Colocasia esculenta*
Foxglove	*Digitalis purpurea*
Fruit pits and seeds	contain: cyanogenic glycosides
Holly	*Ilex*
Ivy	*Hedera*
Iris	*Iris*
Jerusalem cherry	*Solanum pseudocapsicum*
Jimson weed	*Datura stramonium*
Lantana	*Lantana camara*
Lily-of-the-valley	*Convalleria majalis*
Mayapple	*Podophyllum peltatum*
Mistletoe	*Viscum album*
Morning glory	*Ipomoea*
Mountain laurel	*Kalmia iatifolia*
Nightshade	*Salanum spp.*
Oleander	*Nerium oleander*
Peace lily	*Spathiphyllum*
Philodendron	*Philodendron*
Pokeweed	*Phytolacca americana*
Pothos	*Epipremnum aureum*
Yew	*Taxus*

APPENDIX J
HORTICULTURAL GLOSSARY
(AS USED IN THE MANUAL)

- BULB: A storage organ that usually grows underground and often sends out a bloom stalk.

- CALYX: The outer whorl of sepals at the base of flower petals.

- CELL PACK: Usually a six-celled container that holds bedding plants.

- CHARCOAL: Horticultural grade or aquarium charcoal is used in projects such as terrariums to keep soil sweet.

- COTYLEDONS: The first leaves to show on a seedling.

- CUTTING: A piece of a plant used for propagating; often the top 2-inch of a stem consisting of several leaves on top and several bare nodes (bumps where leaves were) on the bottom.

- FERTILIZER: Combination of primarily nitrogen, phosphorous and potassium given to plants to maintain optimal health.

- FLORAL "WET" FOAM: A foam used in floral arranging and sometimes in propagating. It usually comes in a green block, absorbs water and holds flowers.

- GRAVEL: Sterile rock (can be aquarium rock) used in projects such as terrariums, mini-water gardens, fresh flower arrangements.

- HARDY: Refers to plants or bulbs that can survive freezing temperatures.

- NODE: The place on a stem where a leaf either was or will appear. Nodes are where the roots will most often form when a cutting is placed in soil or water.

- OFFSET: A new plant produced naturally by an adult plant, usually at its base.

- PEAT MOSS: An organic material composed of ancient decayed plant material that has been dried and screened. It is a primary component of potting mixes due to its water-holding capacity.

- PERLITE: White volcanic glass that has been heated to a high temperature. The result is a white, very light-weight, porous material that is often a key ingredient in potting mixes. Avoid breathing perlite dust.

- POTTING MIX: A sterile mixture usually consisting of peat moss, vermiculite, and perlite. Other materials that might be included are forest product, topsoil, sand, wetting agent, and time-released fertilizer.

- PRICKING OFF: The process of transferring seedlings from where they were sown into other individual containers, as done in the *Transplanting Seedlings* activity, page 77.

- PROPAGATE, PROPAGATION: The process of starting new plants. Sexual propagation is by seed. Asexual propagation is by cuttings, division, offsets.

- ROOTING HORMONE: This is a product that when placed on the cut end of a hard-to-root cutting,

- ROOTING HORMONE: This is a product that when placed on the cut end of a hard-to-root cutting, stimulates root production and protects from disease.

- SAND: Sterile sand is used in potting mixes for succulents and sometimes used in place of perlite in general potting mixes. It can be found in nurseries.

- SEEDING MIX: A mixture of finely screened peat moss and vermiculite. Ideally, it holds moisture yet will drain well and has no large pieces to interrupt seed growth.

- SEPAL: A part of the calyx — usually green.

- SPHAGNUM MOSS: A green moss that is very absorbent. Often used to line hanging baskets; also makes an excellent mulch in potted plants.

- SUCCULENT: A plant that stores water in its fleshy stem and leaves. All cacti are succulents but not all succulents are cacti.

- TENDER: Refers to plants/bulbs that cannot survive a period of frost.

- TERRARIUM: A self-contained plant environment.

- TIME-RELEASE FERTILIZER: Fertilizer that will continue to feed plants for up to 3-4 months after applied. Excellent idea for outdoor gardens.

- TRUE LEAVES: The second set of leaves to appear on a new seedling. These leaves will actually have the distinguishing features of the mature plant. When the first set of true leaves appear, it is time to transplant seedlings.

- VERMICULITE: The layered clay, mica, heated to a high temperature resulting in a puffy, very absorbent material that is often an ingredient in potting mixes. Also used to cover seeds in seeding projects and as a water and plant holding medium in the *Fresh Flower Mandalas* activity, page 119.

- WATER CYCLE: The process in which water is warmed by the sun, evaporates, condenses, and then precipitates back to the ground to start the cycle over.

APPENDIX K
THERAPEUTIC GLOSSARY

- ADLs: Activities of Daily Living. Physical ADLs (most common in LTC) are basic personal-care tasks including bathing, dressing, eating, transferring from bed or chair, walking, getting outside, using the toilet.

- ALZHEIMER'S DISEASE: A common form of dementia of unknown cause, usually starting in late middle age. It is characterized by memory lapses, confusion, emotional instability and progressive loss of mental ability. It is named after Alois Alzheimer, German neurologist, who described it in 1907.

- APHASIA: Communication disorder caused by certain CVA's resulting in a loss or decrease in the ability to express oneself through speech, comprehend the spoken word, read, or write.

- APRAXIA: Inability to carry out, upon request, purposeful coordinated movements without impairment of muscles or senses.

- AT: Art Therapy

- ATAXIA: Inability to coordinate voluntary muscular movement, which is also symptomatic of some nervous disorders.

- CARF: The Commission on Accreditation of Rehabilitation Facilities

- C/O: Complains of

- COGNITIVE IMPAIRMENT: Affects the ability to think, concentrate, formulate ideas, reason, and remember. It is distinct from a learning disability insofar as it may have been acquired later in life due to injury or illness.

- CP: Cerebral Palsy

- CVA: Cerebralvascular accident (stroke)

- EYE-HAND COORDINATION: Ability to perform activity with the hand using a visual control.

- HEMIANOPSIA (FIELD CUT): Loss of the half of field of vision in one or both eyes following a CVA.

- HEMIPLEGIA: Paralysis of one side of the body and extremities resulting from injury to the brain.

- HI: Hearing Impairment

- JCAHO: Joint Commission on Accreditation of Healthcare Organizations

- LABILITY: Emotional instability that manifests in inappropriate laughing or crying.

- LTC: Long-Term Care

- LTG: Long-Term Goal

- MI: Mental Illness

- MS: Multiple Sclerosis

- MT: Music Therapy

- NEGLECT: Lack of awareness of one side of body and space, usually from a right CVA.

- OT: Occupational Therapy

- P/D: Per Day

- PT: Physical Therapy

- PARAPLEGIA: Symmetrical paralysis of both lower extremities.

- QUADRIPLEGIA: Paralysis of all four extremities.

- RO: Reality Orientation

- RT: Recreation Therapy

- ROM: Range of Motion

- SNF: Skilled Nursing Facility

- STAT: Immediately

- STG: Short-Term Goal

- UNIVERSAL CUFF: An adaptive device worn on the hand to hold items such as utensils, assisting a patient with a weak grasp to participate more in self-care.

- VI: Visual Impairment

- W/C: Wheel Chair

APPENDIX L
PROGRAM ENHANCEMENT IDEAS

Music and Movement
Including music in the garden program whenever possible is a way to enhance outcomes. Older adults enjoy singing the "good old" songs. It's fun to name and sing flower songs such as:
- *Daisy, Daisy*
- *My Wild Irish Rose*
- *Yellow Rose of Texas*
- *When You Wore a Tulip*
- *In the Garden*
- *Mares Eat Oats*

It's also fun to take a familiar tune and create your own words and movements to go along with it, such as the example below that would be suitable for intergenerational or children's programs:

The Garden Song
(to the tune of *The Hokey Pokey*)
You put the shovel in
(pretend to be digging a shovel into the ground)
You pull the rocks out
(bend over, pretend to grab a rock and toss it)
You put the seed in
(hold seed in fingers, bend over, place seed in ground)
And you pat it all about
(patting motion with hands)
You add a little water
(pour from make-believe water can)
And you wait for it to sprout
(arm rises vertically)
And that's what it's all about...
(hands on hips and turn around)
OUR GARDEN!
(clap hands)

Spirituality
One cannot work within the people/plant arena and not begin to see connection after connection to something beyond this physical, 3-dimensional plane of existence. There is an orderliness in nature that we can look at and draw upon to release anxiety, fear or desperation, and to know that the same beauty and rhythm is within us as well.

Some ways of incorporating more of that spiritual connection in the horticultural-based program could be:
- Creating *Fresh Flower Mandalas*, page 119.
- Planting bulbs. Bulbs are the perfect plants for denoting the beauty that comes from within (*Bulb Beauties*, page 97).
- Starting from seed (*Plants from Seeds*, page 73), forcing flowering branches and stem propagation (*New From Old*, page 89), are all ways of acknowledging and honoring the life force within.
- Ceremonies such as Planting Dreams. At a time of planting seeds, have each participant share at least one dream. Involve each person in planting actual seeds, sharing the idea that they are also planting their dreams. Dreams, just like seeds, need to be planted in fertile soil (minds) and cared for lovingly and consistently. Not all seeds germinate and not all dreams come to fruition. When a seed

does not grow, you replant. When a dream does not come to be, you can make adjustments and plant another dream.

- Celebrations of Life that can easily be done during times such as: First blooms of spring, First seeds sprouted from a planting, First harvest.

Outings

Community integration is one of the benefits of incorporating horticulture into programming. Some ways in which to maximize on that benefit are outings to:

- Nurseries/garden centers
- Parks/nature trails
- Botanic gardens/arboretums
- Farmers' markets
- Arbor Day/Earth Day events
- County fairs

Food

"If you feed them they will come" is a true statement. Do you want people to come out of the woodwork to see what's happening? Do you want more staff participation? Try incorporating some cooking sessions with your program.

In the summer garden, it would be as easy as cutting up ripe tomatoes to share or bring along an electric fry pan and sauté tomatoes, onions and summer squash, or prepare fried green tomatoes. In the winter, a nice break is to have fresh fruit, such as pineapple, mango and tangerines, and create a kitchen gardening program that can cover a minimum of two sessions (*Hawaiian Hour I* and *II*, pages 141 and 145).

A key element here is to involve the participants in as much of the prep and serving as possible. Always remember to check for dietary restrictions and follow food safety guidelines.

Reading and Language Activities

Story Time: This is a fun activity for almost any age. Create a story that tells about something that the group has experienced. Examples could be preparing and planting the garden, harvesting the garden, houseplants around the home, etc. Every time the story line comes to a term that the group should know, leave it blank. Provide each participant with a "word bank" made up of all the missing words in the story. As you read the story, participants fill in the blanks by stating the missing word. Below is an example of such a story.

In May, we started our garden. First, we loosened the _____ in the raised beds and pots. Then we added a time-release _____ that would feed the plants from May through August. After we raked the soil even we were ready to plant. In some pots we used _____ to dig deep holes for tomato plants. In one of the raised beds, we made shallow furrows and planted bean _____. We planted borders of pretty yellow and orange flowers called _____. After all the planting was done, we _____ everything with our new coiled hose. We can't wait to harvest our first red ripe _____.

Word Bank:

tomatoes, soil, watered, trowels, seeds, marigolds, fertilizer

Poetry: This can be done indoors or outdoors. It is best to do it where there are not a lot of distractions. Have the group create a poem together. Do not worry about trying to make it rhyme. Use either a flip chart or a dry-erase board to write on, using bold, dark pens. Set a topic such as spring, harvest time, rain, butterflies, etc., and encourage people to share their thoughts. You will be amazed at what they create. Display the completed poem where others can see it when finished.

Getting to Know You: This interactive project is ideal for individuals with good reading skills. It helps people to know one another better and is especially good when bringing two groups together as in an intergenerational program. Pair up people and provide each with pens or pencils and a list of the questions below. Partner A is to ask Partner B the questions and fill in the answers. Then Partner B will do the same with Partner A. In situations where reading skills are minimal or non-existent, the facilitator can ask the questions and write in the answers. A book could be made from individuals' answers, creating a helpful guide for family and visitor discussion topics.

Getting to know you questions:
- What is your favorite flower?
- What is one thing you like about gardening?
- What is your favorite flower color?
- What is your favorite vegetable?
- How do you like that vegetable prepared or cooked?
- Do you like bugs or insects?
- If yes, name one you especially like.
- Did you ever garden with a family member (father, mother, grandparent)?

APPENDIX M
TIPS FOR THE PLANT PROGRAM

- Water Bottles: Use recycled drinking water bottles for plant watering. They are just the right weight for young and old to hold, they provide hand exercise, and they are free!

- Another easy way for some to water is to moisten a clean sponge and have the person watering squeeze the sponge over the planter. This is gentle watering and is especially helpful when caring for newly seeded pots.

- Do not have the budget to buy pots? Use plastic cups. Remember to add either a layer of stones or gravel, or cut holes in the bottom of the cup, to provide proper drainage.

- When purchasing potting mix for all but succulents, select one that is high in peat moss or coconut fiber and low in what is called "forest product." This ensures better water-holding capacity.

- Always moisten dry potting mix with warm water before using. The peat moss in the mixture will absorb warm much more readily than cold water. You will know the mix is damp enough when it is evenly dark in color and it keeps its shape when squeezed. If water drips when squeezing, the mix is too wet. To remedy this problem, add more dry mix. Soil that is too wet has a tendency to compact, impacting the soil aeration required by plants.

- Store dampened potting mix in a well aerated container. If stored in a tightly sealed container, the mixture will mold. One easy way to provide enough air is to drill a number of ½-inch holes in the lid of a rubberized plastic storage container and along the top 2 inches of the container itself. If those using the mix have severely compromised immune systems (cancer patients, for example) always use fresh mix that has not been moistened in the past.

- A greenhouse, or even fancy full-spectrum grow lights, are not necessary to have an indoor plant program. A simple and affordable way to provide light for your plants is to set up a home-made light cart made with a 4-foot long "shop" light. Fluorescent bulbs, one cool white and one warm white, will provide the blue/green spectrum that green foliage plants and African Violets love. Plants do best when they are no more than 12 inches from the light. When building the light cart, create a means for raising and lowering the light fixture. Add a heavy-duty timer, set for 12 hours of light (6:00 a.m. to 6:00 p.m.), to the light fixture's electrical cord. Plug it in and you are ready to grow.

- Plant labels can be re-used if you use pencil instead of pen. Water-proof markers, if used, can be erased using rubbing alcohol.

- Always be sure the pots you use are clean. Dirty pots are one way of spreading disease and insect problems.

- Keep the plant cart clean of debris and avoid crowding plants. Decaying leaves and lack of air flow around the plants are two sure ways of bringing in insect and disease problems.

- Introduce yourself at local florists and nurseries. They might share free or discounted product with you.

- Always thoroughly check donated plants for insect problems. Using a magnifying glass, look at both the undersides and the tops of leaves and along the stems. For minor infestations, douse the plants in insecticidal soap. Discard plants with severe infestations.

APPENDIX N
PLANT NAMES AS USED IN MANUAL

Common Name	Botanical Name
African violet	*Saintpaulia ionantha*
Aloe	*Aloe* spp.
Alyssum	*Alyssum*
Amaryllis	*Hippeastrum* hybrids
Banana	*Musa* sp.
Basil	*Ocimum basilicum*
Begonia	*Begonia* spp.
Busy Lizzie	*Impatiens*
Carnation	*Dianthus caryophyllus*
Cedar	*Cedrus* spp.
Cockscomb	*Celosia* spp.
Chives	*Allium schoenoprasum*
Coleus	*Coleus blumei*
Crocus	*Crocus* sp.
Cypress	*Cupressus* spp.
Daffodil	*Narcissus* spp.
Daisy (Shasta)	*Leucanthemum*
Dill	*Anethum graveolens*
Dusty miller	*Senecio cineraria*
Echeveria	*Echeveria* spp.
Geranium	*Pelargonium* spp.
Hibiscus	*Hibiscus* sp.
Hyacinth	*Hyacinthus orientalis*
Inch plant/spiderwort	*Tradescantia* spp.
Jade plant	*Crassula argentea*
Lavender	*Lavandula angustifolia*
Locust	*Robinia* spp.
Mango	*Mangifera indica*

Common Name	Botanical Name
Marigold	*Tagetes* spp.
Mum	*Chrysanthemum* spp.
Nerve plant	*Fittonia verschaffeltii*
Panda	*Kalanchoe tomentosa*
Pansy	*Viola* spp.
Papaya	*Carica papaya*
Paper white narcissus	*Narcissus tazetta*
Parsley	*Petroselinum crispum*
Peperomia	*Peperomia obtusifolia*
Pepper	*Capsicum annuum*
Pineapple	*Ananas comosus*
Polka dot plant/freckle face	*Hypoestes phyllostachya*
Pumpkin	*Cucurbita* 'Jack-Be-Little'
Purple cup flower	*Nierembergia*
Rose	*Rosa* spp.
Rosemary	*Rosemarinus officinalis*
Scented geranium	*Pelargonium* spp.
Spider plant	*Chlorophytum comosum*
Statice	*Limonium*
Strawflower	*Helichrysum bracteatum*
Sunflower	*Helianthus* spp.
Swedish ivy	*Plectranthus australis*
Thyme	*Thymus* spp.
Tomato	*Lycopersicon* spp.
Tulip	*Tulipa* spp.
Weeping fig	*Ficus benjamina*
Wheat	*Triticum aestivum*
Window pane plant	*Haworthia* spp.
Zebra haworthia	*Haworthia faxciata*
Zinnia	*Zinnia* spp.

ABOUT THE AUTHOR

Pam Catlin, a registered horticultural therapist, has been working in the field of horticultural therapy for over thirty years. During this period of time, she was instrumental in developing over 50 horticultural therapy programs in Washington, Oregon, Illinois, and Arizona. She has practiced horticultural therapy in a variety of settings, including physical rehabilitation, pediatric and psychiatric hospitals, skilled nursing and assisted living centers, memory care communities, adult day programs, and services for those with developmental disabilities. Pam currently serves as the Director of Horticultural Therapy with Adult Care Services, Inc., in Prescott, Arizona. She is on the faculty of the HT Institute, based in Denver, Colorado, and serves as a college mentor in the area of Horticultural Therapy. She is a member of the American Horticultural Therapy Association (AHTA) and has been a regular presenter at AHTA and other conferences. Pam has authored chapters in the books *Horticulture as Therapy: Principles and Practice* (Simson & Straus) and *Horticultural Therapy Methods; Making Connections in Health Care, Human Service, And Community Programs* (Haller & Kramer).

Made in the USA
Charleston, SC
23 August 2012